THE WHICH? GUIDE TO
PAINTING
&
DECORATING

THE WHICH? GUIDE TO
PAINTING
&
DECORATING

Technical consultants: Chris Mortimer & Clive Collins

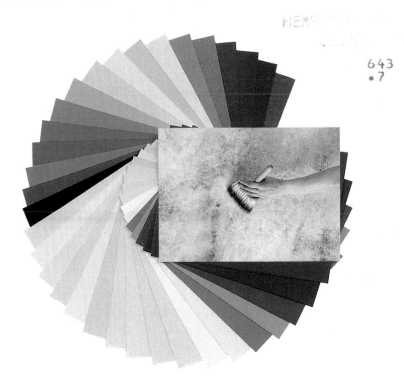

WHICH?
BOOKS

Published by Consumers' Association and Hodder & Stoughton

Which? Books are commissioned by the Association for Consumer Research and published by Consumers' Association, 2 Marylebone Road, London NW1 4DF, and Hodder & Stoughton, 47 Bedford Square, London WC1B 3DP.

The Which? Guide to Painting and Decorating was conceived and produced by Michael Stephenson Publishing. It was designed by Casebourne Rose Design Associates and set by Millhouse Limited, London.

Line Illustrations by Sue Rose.

British Library Cataloguing-in-Publication data:

Which? Guide to Painting and Decorating I. Collins, Clive II. Mortimer, Chris 698

ISBN 0-340 57274-4

First published 1993

Thanks for choosing this book...
If you find it useful, we'd like to hear from you. Even if it doesn't live up to your expectations or do the job you were expecting, we'd still like to know. Then we can take your comments into account when preparing similar titles or, indeed, the next edition of the book. Address your letter to the Publishing Manager at Consumers' Association, FREEPOST, 2 Marylebone Road, London NW1 4DF.
We look forward to hearing from you.

Photographic acknowledgements

Bernard J. Arnull & Co. Ltd cover (centre right)
Crown Paints 55 (bottom), cover (centre left)
Cuprinol 7, 111, cover (bottom right)
L. G. Harris 45 (top)
John Oliver title page (swatch)
Osborne & Little 15, 107 (left)
Sanderson 14, 78, 79, 107 (right)
Sandtex 45 (bottom), cover (bottom left)
Jeremy Thomas title page (centre), 62, 63, 66, 67, 70 71, 74, 75, cover (bottom centre)
Welbeck Golin Harris/Communications Ltd 10, 11
Elizabeth Whiting Associates 51, 54, 55 (top), 58, 59, 98, 102
Zefa 50, 99, 110
Photographic research by Jan Croot.

Printed in Great Britain by Scotprint Ltd., Musselburgh

CONTENTS

INTRODUCTION

The heat of a kitchen is effectively countered by these cool and calming colours. The slightly hard light of the reflective whites has been enhanced by the textured finish of the walls.

Recent research has shown that over half of us undertake our own painting and decorating at one time or another. Often, you can save considerable amounts of money by tackling the job yourself rather than paying professionals. Another reason why DIY can be preferable to hiring professionals (which can itself be a risky business, unless you know your chosen firm to be thoroughly reliable) is that you are naturally more concerned about your property than an outsider, and will probably be prepared to work just a little harder and take just that bit more care. And in addition to questions of cost and quality, doing the work yourself means the satisfaction of a job well done.

There is one snag, though. Inexperience can cost you money and time, compromise quality and may even put you in danger. The temptation is to say to ourselves, 'Anyone can paint and wallpaper', and plunge straight in without proper preparation or understanding. It is usually only when you are precariously perched at the top of a swaying ladder and festooned with yards of pasted wallpaper that you realise there might be a bit more to this business than enthusiasm.

The Which? Guide to Painting & Decorating draws on the skills of experts who have spent their working lives as professional painters and decorators as well as teachers, and the data derived from product-testing carried out by *Which?* magazine. Information on exterior paints, hazardous chemicals in painting products, types of edging floor sanders, interior paints and scaffolding towers is also based on *Which?* findings.

The first chapter states some ground rules about colour, light, pattern and space to help you make better design choices and help prevent costly mistakes. An understanding of, for example, the relationship between colour, room size and shape, light sources, 'cold' and 'warm' colours, pattern and texture will enable you to devise the most effective decorative scheme for the space you are hoping to transform.

Further chapters contain easy-to-follow step-by-step illustrations and colour photographs that take you through every stage of the job: the tools you will need for each painting or decorating task; preparing surfaces properly in order to ensure the best results from your materials; the professional way to paint, hang different types of wallcovering, achieve sophisticated special paint effects such as marbling, stencilling, dragging, ragging and colour-washing; stripping and sealing floors; tiling walls and floors; affixing period features such as ceiling roses, dado rails and cornices, and tackling the outside of your home all the way up from ground to gutter. Tips on estimating quantities or materials, the time each task will take and setting up the work area safely and efficiently appear throughout *The Which? Guide to Painting & Decorating*.

TECHNICAL CONSULTANTS

Chris Mortimer is a professional paint technique consultant. She has used her experience of special paint techniques such as marbling, rag-rolling, stippling, woodgraining, stencilling and dragging on a wide range of domestic and commercial properties, including nightclubs, pubs, shops – and even a nunnery. She teaches special paint techniques at her studio in Brighton – not only to amateurs but also to professional painters and decorators.

Clive Collins runs his own painting and decorating business and has worked on a number of prestige projects, including the complete redecoration of the President of Uganda's State House. Clive also teaches City & Guilds Painting and Decorating at Northbrook College, Worthing.

COLOUR

Many of us are a little intimidated by colour in our homes. The safest bet too often seems to be something non-commital, such as the ubiquitous magnolia or a neutral beige. And to add to our dilemma, paint manufacturers have expanded the range of colours available (and the fanciful names for them) by leaps and bounds over the past years. Faced with hundreds of sample colour cards it is all too easy to become a little colour blind.

Although choosing a colour scheme is above all a matter of personal taste, where one person's 'Autumn Burnish' is another's 'Boring Beige', there are a few basic guidelines about how colour works which will make colour selection less hit-and-miss than it might otherwise be. Above all, though, the use of colour in our homes is a personal expression. Guidelines are just that, guidelines rather than hard-and-fast rules. If you want to experiment work with the largest samples of paint and wallcovering you can. Give yourself time before making a commitment.

The language of colour

The source of all colours are red, blue and yellow (PRIMARY colours). When any two primary colours are mixed in equal proportion they produce a SECONDARY colour. Red and blue produce violet; blue and yellow produce green; red and yellow

produce orange. Two secondary colours mixed together will give a TERTIARY colour. The colour wheel shows the relationship of the 12 basic permutations of primary, secondary and tertiary colours, although the number of permutations is almost inexhaustible. The 12 colours of our colour wheel are known as TRUE colours or HUES. Their colour VALUE is a measure of their closeness to the primary colours; the closer they are, the more intense they appear. Their TONE (relative lightness or darkness) can be controlled by diluting them with white to produce a TINT or deepening them with black to produce a SHADE. The colour bar shows the effect of lightening blue to a tint and of darkening it to a shade.

The colour wheel is arranged to show COMPLEMENTARY colours (those that face each other on opposite points of the wheel) and RELATED colours (those that lie next to each other on the wheel).

If complementary colours are mixed they tend to neutralise each other. But if used judiciously together they can create striking accents. If, for example, walls and ceiling were painted in related tones of orange, a feature such as a dado rail could be effectively picked out in the complementary colour to orange, which is blue.

Related colours are those most often used in conjunction in a colour scheme. They give consistency and co-ordination to a room, but if they are used unimaginatively they can also create a dreary conformity. Related colour schemes need to have a little drama, possibly a strong feature accented in a complementary colour.

Above: *The natural light in this cottage interior has been enhanced by the use of a monotone colour scheme of shades of white. This has the effect of appearing to raise the beams of the ceiling, making the room seem larger.* Left: *The richly glowing collection of patterns which decorate this town sitting-room have been skilfully united by sponging the walls with a warm apricot colour.*

Colour wheel

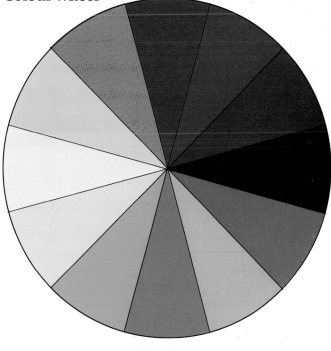

THE PSYCHOLOGY OF COLOUR

It is not necessary to understand the complex science of the psychology of colour to know intuitively how colours influence our feelings. Certain colours will make us feel bright and happy; others reflective and tranquil, while yet others will make us edgy and uncomfortable.

WARM AND COOL

Colours in the yellow/red sector of the wheel are known as 'warm' and can make a room feel welcoming and cosy. They also tend to make a space feel smaller and more intimate. The more intense the colour, the more exciting the effect. The more subdued the tone, the more comfortable the ambience.

Research has shown that people actually feel warmer in rooms decorated with reds, yellows or oranges, so they are effective colours to use in cold rooms, or north-facing rooms that receive colder light.

'Cool' colours fall in the blue/green sector of the wheel. Intense cool colours are attention-catching and fresh, while their more subdued versions, such as greys, are tranquil and restful. Cool colours are particularly effective in south-facing rooms which receive a compensating warm-toned sunlight. Rooms decorated in cool colours have a greater sense of space and formality.

COLOUR AND SPACE

Colour can change our perception of space. As a rule lighter colours tend to enhance the feeling of space because they create an illusion of receding surfaces. Darker and bolder colours, on the other hand, draw attention to surfaces and pull in walls and ceilings. Dark colours are also useful in helping to disguise problems such as uneven walls or areas of heavy wear and tear because they absorb light rather than reflect it from the blemish.

Finishes will also affect our perception of space. A high-gloss finish reflects more light and therefore draws attention to surfaces, making a room feel smaller. Matt finishes do not reflect as much light and therefore make the planes of walls and ceilings appear to recede.

The perception of a room's height is influenced by the counterplay between the colour of the walls and ceiling. The darker the ceiling by comparison to the wall colour, the lower the ceiling appears. Dark walls and a light ceiling increase the sense of height.

HIDING AND HIGHLIGHTING

The ugly radiator or the gorgeous moulding can be hidden or highlighted by a judicious use of colour. Painting skirtingboard or featureless and uninteresting doors, for example, in the same colour as the walls will help 'lose' these unsightly features. It will also increase the feeling of space in a small room. On the other hand, a dado rail, for example, picked out in a complementary colour to the wall will highlight the feature and create the illusion of bringing in the walls by drawing attention to them.

COLOUR AND LIGHT

The effect of light on colour will have such an important impact on the final look you are striving to achieve that it is worth thinking about the light sources in your home before you settle on any particular decorative scheme. Does the room get direct or indirect natural light? Which direction does it come from? Is the room one that will be used mainly in the evening or at night – a sitting-room or bedroom, for example? If so, what kind of artificial lighting is used? Before buying paint or wallpaper get as large a sample as you can. Many manufacturers now provide tester cans of paint, enough to paint a good size piece of board (remember to prepare and undercoat the board to get a true effect) or thick white card. Similarly, it is usually possible to get a large swatch of wall paper from your stockist. Hang the samples on the wall to see how they react to different light conditions over a full 24-hour period. If a room is most often used at a particular time of day, look at the colour carefully at that time. Paint and wallpaper will take on a very different character in your home than they do in an artificially lit shop or DIY centre. As with all aspects of decorating, patience and time are the best investments you can make.

NATURAL LIGHT

Colour reflects light, and the types of light sources in the rooms to be decorated will always play an active part in the final effect. The first consideration is the orientation or 'aspect' of your property. The diagram on page 14 summarises the effect of natural light from different directions and at different times of day. For example, a predominantly white colour scheme may appear creamy in a south-facing room receiving warm sunlight, while in a room facing north the same white paint will take on a chillier blue/green tinge. A west-facing room receives the warmer light of afternoon and an east-facing one the colder light of morning, each of which will have its effect on the same white paint.

As a rule of thumb it is advisable to use warm colours in north- and east-facing rooms and cool colours in south- and west-facing rooms.

ARTIFICIAL LIGHT

Tungsten produces a light similar to daylight but tinged with yellow. It emphasises red tones and suppresses blues and greens. There is now a range of soft-tone coloured tungsten bulbs available.

Fluorescent lighting gives a harsh bluish light that tends to reduce shadowing and therefore flattens textures; colours may appear cold and dull. In most homes, however, fluorescent lighting is used in kitchens and utility rooms which are often decorated with cool colours anyway. It is possible now to buy fluorescent tubes with warm light.

Halogen is a fairly recent development in domestic lighting, these small bulbs give off a very intense white light that particularly favours more modernistic interior design schemes that tend to emphasise cool colours, unfussy finishes and geometric lines.

COLOUR AND CONTINUITY

For most of us it is rare indeed to have the luxury of planning a decorative scheme from scratch, complete with new furnishings, carpets, curtains, pictures and ornaments. Mostly we have to work with what we already have.

In order to pull old and new into a coherent design, plan ahead. If possible, take small samples of existing upholstery, carpet and curtains and put them into a folder. You might want to augment the folder with clippings of magazine photographs that have particularly inspired you. Take the folder with you when you visit showrooms and stockists so that you can add paint colour cards and wallcovering swatches. When you have assembled your sample folder spread it out at home in the room you want to decorate. Imagine how new colours and patterns will work with existing furnishing and, above all, take your time.

PATTERN, COLOUR AND SPACE

The prospect of choosing a patterned wall-covering can be as daunting as selecting a colour scheme. But, as with colour, pattern has the power to increase the sense of space and is a very valuable design tool. Again, a few simple guidelines will help:
* Smaller-scale patterns help to increase the sense of space.
* Larger-scale patterns tend to 'advance' a surface and make the space feel smaller.
* A light-coloured background will increase the sense of space. Even a small-patterned wallcovering on a dark background will make a room look smaller.
* To prevent a room looking too 'boxy' choose a pattern with an open, light and airy background. The eye will look through and beyond the pattern thus making the space appear larger. Picking out a wall in a different colour to the rest will also make a room look less 'boxy'.
* Vertical stripes or bands of pattern on a wall will create the illusion of a higher ceiling.
* Horizontal stripes or bands of colour on a wall will make a wall look wider.

The wide-awake boldness of this kitchen makes dramatic use of the light source and has been achieved with a single colour and pattern.

Before decorating a room it is worth considering the effects of sunlight on colours. Light from the north and east tends to give a colder cast, while light from the south and west is warmer.

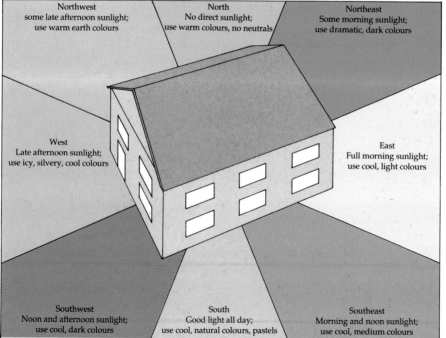

Northwest
some late afternoon sunlight;
use warm earth colours

North
No direct sunlight;
use warm colours, no neutrals

Northeast
Some morning sunlight;
use dramatic, dark colours

West
Late afternoon sunlight;
use icy, silvery, cool colours

East
Full morning sunlight;
use cool, light colours

Southwest
Noon and afternoon sunlight;
use cool, dark colours

South
Good light all day;
use cool, natural colours, pastels

Southeast
Morning and noon sunlight;
use cool, medium colours

TEXTURE

Texture refers to how paint or wall-covering feels (or looks as though it would feel) to the touch. Texture can be created two-dimensionally, as with tightly repeating small-patterned wallcovering, or three-dimensionally, as with raised-pattern wallcoverings or paint containing gritty particles.

Apart from their purely aesthetic appeal, textured finishes are useful for hiding blemishes such as damaged or badly executed plasterwork or a wall with slight bulges or indentations. Because textured surfaces reflect light from multiple facets and angles they divert attention away from an underlying surface flaw.

In most cases textured surfaces tend to bring in walls and ceilings, giving the illusion of less space. They work best as accents (highlights of smaller areas that will act as focal points) rather than used over large expanses where they can be overwhelming.

The strong sunlight flooding through the windows warms and softens the medley of cool greens.

PAINTING INTERIORS

The development of modern paints has transformed DIY interior decoration. On the aesthetic level, the range of colours, sheens and textures is staggering, and in combination opens up a tremendous spectrum of choices. On the practical level, the increased versatility of modern paints, with their enhanced coverage rates, drying times and opacity, as well as their dripless and virtual odourless characteristics, make home decorating much quicker, cleaner and less uncomfortable than it has ever been.

However, confidence in these qualities can also create a tendency to rush into the job. The amount of time spent preparing the surface to be painted will pay huge dividends in the quality of the final effect, and the better organised we are before we pick up brush, pad or roller, the more will be saved in time, money and frayed nerves.

wrong

right

A simple and safe platform made of scaffold-board securely fastened to stepladders.

SAFETY

LADDER SENSE

Year after year falls from ladders are a leading cause of household injuries. Here are some guidelines that will help reduce the chances of a mishap.

* When buying a ladder or using one for the first time read the manufacturer's sticker attached to one of the legs. The sticker will give weight ratings and instructions for proper use.

* Do not climb any stepladder unless its legs are fully open, the feet firmly grounded, and the spreader bar locked in place.

* Do not use ladders near electrical wires.

* Do not leave ladders unattended when there are children around.

* Do not stand on the top rung, top or utility shelf. The top rung should never come below your waist.

* Do not overreach. Keep your weight centred and move the ladder as frequently as necessary in order to keep within a safe and comfortable distance from your work.

* Keep ladders clean of paint spills to avoid slipping.
* Do not keep tools such as Stanley knives or screwdrivers on the top of a stepladder. They may cause injury if they fall when the ladder is moved.
* When selecting a scaffold-board for bridging between ladders or sawhorses, ensure it is no longer than 12ft (3m). It should be 10in (25cm) wide and 2in (5cm) thick. Choose boards without knots or cracks. The board should have a little spring in it as brittle boards can snap unexpectedly.
* When boards are set between stepladders or across sawhorses the boards should extend 12in (30cm) beyond them.
* If you bridge two stepladders with boards ensure that the steps of the ladders are facing each other.
* Clamp or lash bridging boards to stepladders or sawhorses.

For exterior ladders and towers, see pages 142–147.

head wall

pad top of ladder to avoid damaging the wall

well wall

lash boards together

landing

sawhorse

fix batten to landing to secure steps

A secure platform for working in a stairwell. Note the top of the ladder wrapped in cloths to protect the wall.

Left: *A stair scaffold compensates for the difference in stair heights.*

Right: *An adjustable stair ladder and scaffolding board. Note the ladder secured to the stair with rope.*

PAINT SAFETY

Some paints contain powerful solvents and can be harmful. Here are the main points of paint safety.

* Always read the instructions on paint containers for warnings about possible hazards. Do not take short-cuts – follow the safety instructions.
* Keep paint and paint products such as thinners, varnishes and stripping solutions away from children.
* Keep pets away from painting areas. Birds, in particular, can be seriously affected by paint fumes.
* Always work with paint products in a well-ventilated area. Excessive inhalation of fumes from paint and solvents can cause dizziness, head-aches, nausea and fatigue.
* If you cannot ventilate a room sufficiently wear an approved respirator.
* Wear a dust mask when sanding.
* Wear safety goggles when working with chemical strippers or caustic compounds or painting over-head.
* Wear rubber gloves when working with paint strippers or other caustic products.
* Turn off all sources of flame, including pilot lights, when spraying with any paint containing solvent. Do not smoke when using products containing solvents. In-haling them with hot tobacco smoke makes them even more toxic.
* Oil- or solvent-soaked rags should not be kept, especially in a crumpled state, as there is a risk of spontaneous combustion. Spread the rags out flat so that solvent can evaporate, or keep them in water until they can be safely disposed of.
* When working with highly flammable products keep a foam or dry powder extinguisher nearby.

DEALING WITH LEAD PAINT

Lead-based paints have almost entirely disappeared from the amateur market because of the risk of lead poisoning, especially to young children. If you have any tins of gloss paint or primer more than about six years old they could well contain lead-based pigments. Some modern liquid driers, for example, (solutions added to oil- and alkyd-based paints to speed up their drying time) still contain lead.

Old paintwork may contain lead and should be dealt with carefully in order to avoid the inhalation of air-borne lead-bearing dust particles. If you think the paintwork might contain lead (old gloss paint on woodwork, for example, should be treated with suspicion) take the following precautions:

* Do not use a blowtorch or heat gun for stripping, as the heat may create toxic fumes.
* Do not use dry sandpaper, as it creates fine dust that could be inhaled.
* Do not burn stripped debris. Bag it and dispose of it in a dustbin.
* Wear a dust mask and rubber gloves.

Potentially harmful chemicals in paint products

PAINT AND VARNISH

Chemicals	Found in	Swallowing	Inhalation	Absorption	Corrosive	Irritant	Flammable
2-ethoxyethanol	Paint (cellulose)	–	–	–	no	yes	yes
Ethyl glycol acetate	Paint (cellulose)	●	●	●	no	yes	yes
Isobutanol	Paint (cellulose)	–	–	–	no	yes	yes
Lead (eg calcium plumbate)	*Primer*	●	●	●	no	no	no
Nitrocellulose	Paint (cellulose)	–	–	–	no	no	yes[1]
Organic solvents eg acetone	Lacquers, varnish	●	●	–	no	yes	yes[1]
Trichloroethylene	Paint (hammered enamel) *Paint (gloss)*	–	●	–	no	yes	no
Xylene	Paint (enamel), *paint (gloss)* Paint (cellulose)	●	●	●	no	yes	yes
White spirit	Paint *(gloss)*	●	–	–	no	yes	yes

[1] Highly flammable

PAINT REMOVERS

		Swallowing	Inhalation	Absorption	Corrosive	Irritant	Flammable
Dichloromethane	Paintbrush cleaner, Paint stripper, varnish stripper	–	●	–	no	yes	no
Ethanol	Methylated spirit	●	–	–	no	yes	yes[1]
Methanol	Paint stripper, varnish stripper	●	●	–	no	no	yes[1]
Naphtha	Paint brush cleaner	●	●	●	no	yes	yes
Sodium hydroxide (caustic soda)	Paint stripper	●	–	–	yes	yes	no
Turpentine oil	Turpentine	●	–	–	no	yes	no
Trichloroethylene	*Varnish stripper*	–	●	–	no	yes	no
White spirit		●	–	–	no	yes	yes

[1] Highly flammable
Italics = alternative products available   ● = Potentially dangerous

If an accident happens

SUSPECTED POISONING: Do not try to induce vomiting. If you can swallow easily, drink a glass of milk or water. Go to hospital. Take the offending product with you.
CONTACT WITH CORROSIVES: Act fast. Flush the area with lots of cold water. If skin is damaged or pain persists, go to hospital.
CONTACT WITH IRRITANTS: On the skin: wash well with soapy water. In eyes: flush well with cold water for at least 10 minutes, holding the eyelids apart. If pain persists or inflammation develops, go to hospital.

EQUIPMENT

Although you do not have to break the bank by buying professional-standard equipment (brushes, in particular, can cost a good deal if you buy at the top end of the range) it is worth investing in good-quality equipment that will last and do the job efficiently.

Shavehooks *For scraping paint from the awkwardly angled mouldings of woodwork.*

Filling knives *A 1¹/₂in (38mm) putty knife for general scraping, flaking and wood filling. A 6in (150mm) filling knife for repairing larger areas of damaged plasterwork with filling compound.*

Masking tape *For protecting window pane edges from paint.*

Dusting brush *To remove debris from surface to be painted.*

Work with tough **PVC gloves** *rather than flimsier household rubber gloves for maximum protection from highly caustic liquid paint strippers.*

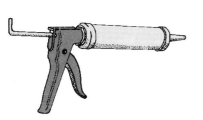

Mastic gun *Tubes of flexible mastic filler are loaded into the barrel and squeezed into those gaps between masonry and woodwork which, if they expanded, would crack rigid fillers.*

Hot-air paint stripper *Much easier to use than the traditional blowtorch. It strips as quickly as a blowtorch but without the risks of scorching the wood or of working with a naked flame.*

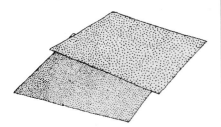

Wet-and-dry paper *For smoothing new paintwork before the final coat. Dip the paper in water and work over the paint surface. Wipe off the paintwork when it is still wet. Rinse the surface well with clean water.*

OTHER USEFUL EQUIPMENT

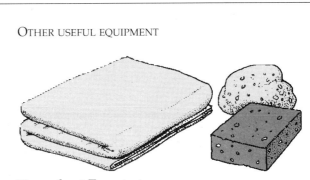

Drop-sheet *To protect furniture and floors from paint drips and spills. Use absorbent canvas cloth rather than plastic sheeting; it is worth the extra cost. Plastic sheets can also be dangerously slippery.*

Sponges *For cleaning up water-based paint drips.*

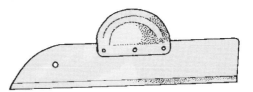

Paint shield *To prevent paint getting on to glass when painting window glazing bars or on to carpet when painting the base of skirtingboard.*

Tack cloth *Lint-free cloth which is tacky (impregnated with linseed oil) and therefore can remove dust from surfaces prior to paintstrip.*

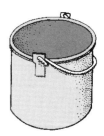

Plastic paint kettle *For mixing and holding more manageable amounts of paint than the manufacturer's tin.*

BRUSHES, ROLLERS AND PADS

BRUSHES

It is worth spending a little more on good-quality brushes. They will not shed as many hairs onto your paint and, if you take care of the brushes as suggested on pages 48-49, will last much longer than cheaper counter-parts.

Use natural bristles to apply alkyd- and oil-based paints. They are less effective with water-based paints because the hairs are hollow and become limp with soaked-up water. A good synthetic filament brush is suitable for all types of paint.

½in (12mm); 1 in (25mm); 2in (50mm) flat brushes for glossing, varnishing and trimming.

Left: 1in (25mm) cutting-in brush with a bevelled edge for working on narrow areas such as glazing bars. 4in (100mm) wall and ceiling brush for covering larger areas. They also come in 5in (125mm), 6in (150mm) and 7in (175mm) widths but these larger sizes can be heavy and difficult to handle when charged with paint.

Radiator brush *When a radiator cannot be removed, this brush (there are also wooden and plastic-handled versions) will let you get to the wall behind the radiator.*

Choosing a brush

* Look for 'flagging': the split end to each bristle, whether natural or synthetic fibre. The more flagging there is, the more paint your brush can hold.
* Look for 'chiselling': the length of the bristles is graduated, which results in the tapering needed to produce a good straight edge.

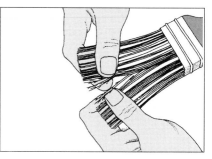

* Flick through the bristles with your thumb. They should be springy and flexible. A little gentle tugging should not dislodge too many bristles.

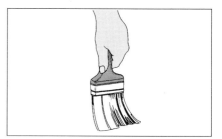

* Spread out the bristles and see if they are well seated in the base. On the best brushes the metal hand or ferrule will be of copper or stainless steel.
* Look at the thickness of the stock of the brush. Paying a little more will buy you a brush with twice the depth of stock compared to an economy brush. The thicker the stock, the more paint the brush can hold and the longer it will last.

ROLLERS

Rollers are particularly efficient for covering large areas.

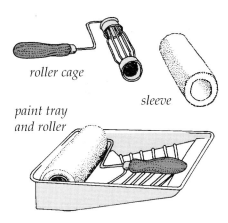

roller cage

sleeve

paint tray and roller

Avoid rollers that require you to unthread a nut in order to secure the sleeve. They are a messy nuisance and often corrode. A roller taking a 9in (225mm) sleeve will handle most jobs. Look for a roller handle that can take a threaded extension pole.

Sleeves are made in lambswool or synthetic fibre. Use a deep-pile sleeve for textured surfaces and medium pile for water-based paints; a short pile is usually used for oil-based paint. Avoid cheap plastic foam which leaves air bubbles in the paint surface.

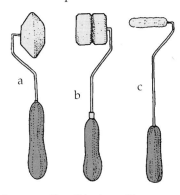

a

b

c

(a) Corner roller, (b) pipe roller, (c) radiator roller.

PAINT PADS

Research undertaken by *Which?* shows that beginners prefer the simplicity of paint pads over brushes or rollers. Pads cover quickly and are less likely to drip than brushes or rollers.

Apply the paint to the wall by smoothing the paint pad across the surface. If you find the paint is streaking you are probably pulling the pad across the surface too quickly. Allowing the loaded pad to stand for too long in one place may also lead to uneven coverage.

Some pads have a hollow handle to accommodate an extension pole to enable you to paint the top of a wall without using a ladder. Clean paint pads as you would a roller (see page 48).

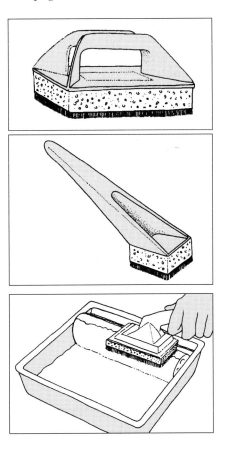

Standard pads in various sizes. The foam-rubber base is covered with mohair pile.

Sash pad for painting glazing bars on windows.

The best pad trays have paint-loading rollers for even distribution across the pad.

PAINTS

Paint is made up of pigment (tiny particles of minerals, chemicals or metals) that give the paint its colour or determine the density of its whiteness. Binders (resins) enable the pigment to bind to the surface to be painted. Originally, binders were made from the natural secretions of plants and insects, but now are made from chemicals such as alkyds, acrylics, vinyls and urethanes. Binders and pigments are held in a solution of water (for emulsion paints) or spirit (for oil paints) that allows them to be spread easily onto the surface. In addition, paints contain driers – chemicals that speed up the drying process and, sometimes, extenders such as chalk or talc to increase the opacity of the paint.

For most interior jobs the choice is between emulsion or oil-based paints. Oil-based paints have a very high resin content and dry to a tough finish, so they are mainly used on woodwork and metal. To use them over large areas such as walls and ceilings is expensive and, in addition, the glossiness of an oil paint finish tends to highlight any irregularities in the surface. Emulsion paint, on the other hand, has a relatively large amount of pigments and extenders which dry to a more matt finish, (and the less reflective the surface, the less pronounced are the surface imperfections). Emulsion paints are also cheaper than oils and therefore more cost-effective in covering larger areas.

LABELLING

Always read the manufacturer's label. It should tell you the surfaces for which the paint is best suited, and what appropriate primer/sealers and undercoat (if any) should be used first. It should also tell you the covering rate (how many square metres the contents of the tin will cover), approximate drying time, and whether there are any hazards, such as inflammability and toxicity, associated with the paint.

ONE COAT OR TWO?

Most of us are keen to minimise the cost of our redecoration, but sometimes the savings implied in economy paints are not realised because more paint is needed to achieve a satisfactory finish. Cheap paint does not have the same amount of pigments as good-quality paint and therefore cannot give as dense a coverage.

One-coat paints cover a smaller area than their traditional two-coat counterparts, and usually cost more per tin. However, the opacity of one-coat paints was found in *Which?* tests to be the equal of two-coat paints – and, of course, they also save on time and effort. The choice between one- or two-coat paint depends to some extent on the underlying colour you need to cover. If it is a strong colour, then use a one-coat paint; if it is a light colour you will probably find that a traditional emulsion will do the job more economically.

PRIMER/SEALERS

A sealer creates an impermeable membrane between the surface and subsequent coats. It prevents stains such as oil leaching out from the surface, penetrating the paint finish. Primers help to lay down a slightly rough 'footing' for the final coats that helps to build up their opacity and covering capability. There are various kinds for different purposes and a good idea is to get advice from your stockist on which is best for the job you have to tackle. For example:

Primer/sealer undercoat: As the name suggests, primer/sealer undercoat does three jobs in one. Use it on wood and plaster. Its acrylic resins are in a water solvent, and water can raise the grain of wood, so rubbing down before and after application may be necessary.

All-purpose primer: Sometimes called universal or multi-purpose primer. It is good on wood, plaster, plasterboard, stone, brick and metal unless there is a particular problem such as rust on metal or bituminous stains in wood or plaster.

Knotting: A shellac varnish based on the secre-

tions of a particular species of beetle. Used to seal the resin that oozes from 'live' wood knots.
Zinc chromate primer: Use on aluminium window frames.
Zinc phosphate primer: Use on ferrous (iron-based) metals.
Red lead: Use on new wood.
Red oxide: A tannate primer sometimes known as 'Rusty'. It deactivates rust.
Stabilising primer: Use on plaster, brick and cement in order to 'fix' any powdery surface.
Alkali-resistant primer: Use on new plaster, cement, concrete or brick before using an oil-based paint that would otherwise react badly with the alkali deposits in the material to be painted.
Aluminium wood primer: Use on hardwoods that tend to have a high natural oil content, also on softwoods that are high in natural resins or on woods that have been creosoted or scorched during heat-stripping.

EMULSION PAINT

The basic paint for covering walls and ceilings, emulsion is water-based with either vinyl or acrylic resins to bond the pigment. The traditional choice is between matt or silk finish. Matt generally has a better hiding power than silk and is particularly useful if the surface to be painted has slight blemishes. The glossier the paint, the more the blemishes will show. Silk emulsions, though, have a better resistance to washing and are more suitable for use in, say, children's rooms, bathrooms, or kitchens.

Some manufacturers offer a 'satin' finish which is somewhere between matt and silk in appearance. It does not have the same opacity as silk or matt paint, so it won't hide underlying colours as effectively. Specialist kitchen and bathrooms paints also failed to cover as effectively as matt and silk emulsions in recent *Which?* tests.

Emulsion can be bought in a semi-solid form as well as in traditional liquid. This non-drip form comes in its own tray (for convenient rolling) and, because it is less messy to use than its liquid counterparts, is particularly handy for ceilings.

OIL PAINT

Because oil-based paints dry to a harder finish than emulsion paints they are better for surfaces that are likely to take scuffs and fingering – doors and skirtingboards for example. Good preparation and undercoating are essential for best results, high-gloss paints in particular will show up blemishes dramatically.

The resins that bind the pigment in oil-based paint are either alkyds or the quicker drying polyurethane (which is used mainly on interior wood and metalwork). Non-drip (thixotropic) varieties come in the form of a gel, and are particularly useful for the less-experienced painter as they do not drip or run like liquid gloss. Oil-based paints come in matt, semi-gloss, and full-gloss finishes.

SPECIAL INTERIOR PAINTS

Radiator enamel: Specifically designed not to yellow as does ordinary gloss paint when subjected to heat. Available in gloss or satin finishes.
Anti-condensation paint: Contains particles of clay or vermiculite that insulate the surface and reduce condensation. Useful in kitchens and bathrooms, but its relatively poor coverage rate will increase its costs compared to conventional paints.
Textured paint: Sand-like particles are mixed with emulsion paint to give a rough finish that is particularly useful in masking damage and other surface blemishes. To keep down dust (which tends to collect on textured surfaces) it is advisable to give textured paint a coat of vinyl emulsion. It is worth remembering that textured paint is quite porous, and will require about 25% more emulsion than on an ordinary surface. See page 44 for application.
Fire-retardant paint: An emulsion that produces a foamy insulation when exposed to extreme heat. Particularly useful to paint polystyrene ceiling tiles, which can be highly inflammable. Follow the manufacturer's instructions carefully, and do not cover it with another type of paint that may compromise the fire-retardant paint's effectiveness. It is often advised not to wash fire-retardant paint.

ESTIMATING FOR INTERIORS

The chart below gives approximate covering rates. Check with the estimates on the manufacturer's label. When estimating paint, bear in mind:

* The porosity of the surface. New plaster and textured finishes will need more paint than previously treated or untextured surfaces.
* Thixotropic (dripless) paint covers less area but more densely than its liquid counterpart (see page 25).
* Painting over a dark colour with a lighter colour will often require an extra coat.
* 'Bargain' paints are very often thinner than good-quality brands and may need twice as many coats to cover the same area.
* Adequately seal and undercoat new plaster and wood. It will save you money by cutting down on the number of top coats in more expensive finishing paint.
* Buy a little more paint than you think you will need. You may want to paint the interiors of built-in bookcases, for example, or at some later date need a little paint for touching-up repairs. Apart from the expense of later having to buy a relatively large quantity for a small repair, the colour-matching of a later batch may not be exact.

COVERING RATES, SQUARE METRE PER LITRE*			
	Walls & ceilings	metal	woodwork
Emulsion undercoat	15		
Gloss undercoat	14	16	16
Wood primer			7-8
Metal primer		9-11	
Emulsion	13		
Gloss	9-10	12	12
Eggshell	12	14	14
Wood varnish			16
* 1 sq. metre = 1.196 sq. yards 1 litre = 0.22 gallons			

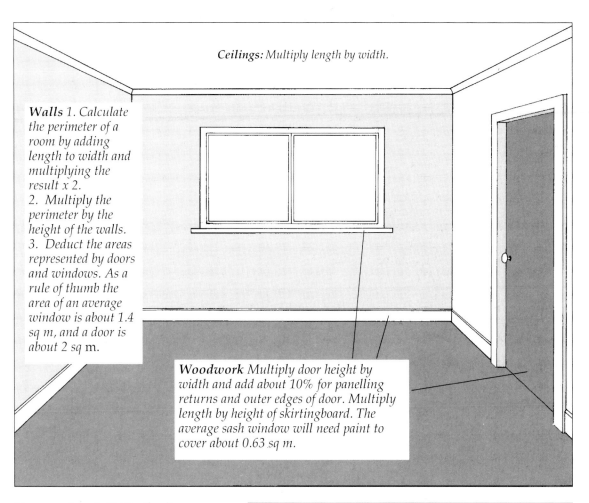

Ceilings: Multiply length by width.

Walls 1. *Calculate the perimeter of a room by adding length to width and multiplying the result x 2.*
2. Multiply the perimeter by the height of the walls.
3. Deduct the areas represented by doors and windows. As a rule of thumb the area of an average window is about 1.4 sq m, and a door is about 2 sq m.

Woodwork *Multiply door height by width and add about 10% for panelling returns and outer edges of door. Multiply length by height of skirtingboard. The average sash window will need paint to cover about 0.63 sq m.*

How much paint? *Use the diagram above to calculate the area to be painted and the amount of paint you will need.*

METRIC CONVERSION TABLE	
To convert:	multiply by:
Inches to centimetres	2.540
Centimetres to inches	0.3937
Feet to metres	0.3048
Metres to feet	3.281
Metres to yards	1.094
Sq. inches to sq. centimetres	6.452
Sq. centimetres to sq. inches	0.1550
Sq. metres to sq. feet	10.76
Sq. feet to sq. metres	0.0929
Sq. yards to sq. metres	0.8361
Gallons to litres	4.546
Litres to gallons	0.22

PREPARING WALLS AND CEILINGS

GETTING READY

It cannot be stressed enough that organisation and preparation are vital to achieve good results. Patience and care spent at the beginning of a job will pay handsome dividends.

General preparation checklist

1. Turn off electricity while you are dealing with light fittings, outlets and switches.

2. Remove cover plates from the switches (returning cover screws to screwholes). Drop light fittings from ceiling and cover with a plastic bag.

3. Unscrew door, window and fitted furniture hardware (keep screws and handles in clearly indentifiable envelopes). Keep the door knob in the room with you in case you are shut in accidentally!

4. Remove all nails, screws, picture hangers etc from walls.

5. Remove as much furniture as possible from the room. Move what remains to the centre and cover with drop sheets. Cover floors with canvas drop sheets.

6. If there is an open fire, have the chimney swept to prevent a soot fall during decorating.

7. Vacuum thoroughly. With bare floorboards, sprinkle with water and sweep up the dust.

8. Dress in old clothes but avoid wearing wool, which can shed fibres onto wet paint. See 'Safety' on page 18 for suggestions on protective clothing.

9. Wash previously painted walls and woodwork using sugar soap. Work in small circular areas from the bottom of the wall to the top, and on ceilings work away from the window (see diagram below). Rinse with clean warm water. For greasy surfaces wipe down with a cloth impregnated with white spirit remembering to extinguish all naked flames, including pilot lights.

Washing down *Work in small circular areas. On walls, start at the bottom and progress to the top. On ceilings, work away from the windows.*

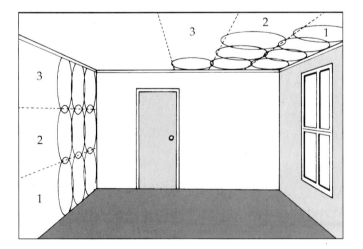

MILDEW

A combination of damp, warmth and poor ventilation can result in a persistent fungal growth known as mildew, which appears on surfaces as sooty specks. First you should correct the conditions that cause mildew growth. Next tackle the spores by washing with a solution of one part household bleach to three parts warm water (wearing rubber gloves). There are also proprietary anti-mildew sprays. Leave the solution for 3-4 hours. Scrape off the spores on to newspaper and burn. Rinse the surface thoroughly with clear warm water. Use primer and paint with an anti-fungal ingredient.

DISTEMPER

A mixture of chalk, size and water, distemper is still occasionally found in older properties. It does not provide a stable base for new decorations and should be removed

With a stiff brush remove as much loose distemper as possible and wash off the rest with clear warm water with a little wallpaper stripper added. Over years of distempering, the detailing of plaster moulding often becomes clogged. With patience the distemper can be removed using a toothbrush and water/ stripper solution. Stabilise the surface of cleaned distemper with an all-purpose primer.

PAINTING OVER WALLPAPER

As a base for paint, old wallpaper is only as solid as its adhesive. If moisture (from emulsion paint, for example) weakens the paste, the old paper will bubble or peel away.

Vinyl-coated papers should have the coating stripped off to reveal the backing paper. Where paper is badly torn or missing, flake off any peeling edges and apply a light coat of filler. Allow to dry and lightly sand until it is smooth to the touch. If the pattern is bright, it is best to seal the paper with an all-purpose primer.

DEALING WITH PLASTER

New plaster: Must be given time to dry thoroughly, which may take six weeks. Some paints will lose their opacity and even flake off if they are applied to insufficiently cured plaster. During the drying process alkaline deposits (efflorescence) will leach out on to the plaster's surface.

Remove these deposits periodically with a stiff brush. If the deposits keep on returning you have a damp problem which needs to be cured at source. Use an alkali-resistant primer if you intend to apply oil paint. If using emulsion, seal the plaster with thinned emulsion to prevent it soaking up too much finishing paint.

Old plaster: If the surface is powdery and friable, seal it with a thinned coat of primer-sealer. Make good any surface defects, rub down with a dusting brush and treat newly plastered patches with a coat of thinned emulsion.

Plasterboard: Fill joints between boards. If applying oil paint, first coat with primer-sealer. If applying emulsion, coat with thinned emulsion.

PATCHING PEELING PAINTWORK

CRACKS IN PLASTER

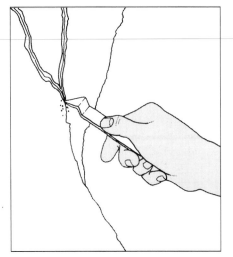

1. Scrape away loose paint with filling knife or paint scraper.

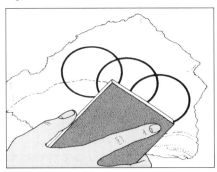

2. Dampen the exposed plaster and fill with compound. Allow compound to dry.

1. Scrape out any loose plaster. Widen hairline cracks a few millimetres to give the filling compound a better purchase. Brush out loose dust.

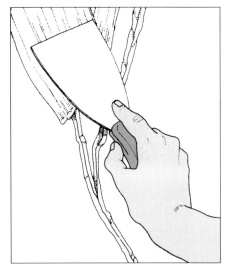

3. Sand the repair using fine sandpaper until the surface is smooth to the touch. Seal the patch with a thinned coat of primer-sealer.

2. Using a filling knife, spread the compound along the length of the crack, pressing it in firmly. Allow the filler to dry for about two hours. If the filling compound has shrunk during this time, apply another layer. When dry, sand with fine sandpaper until smooth to the touch. Seal the repair with a coat of thinned primer-sealer.

LARGER HOLES IN PLASTER

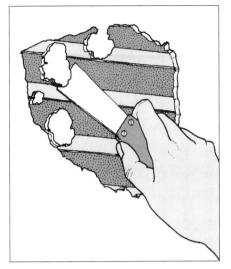

1. Scrape and brush out loose plaster.

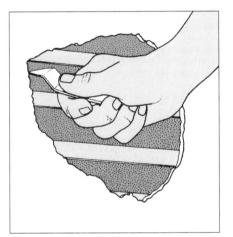

2. Take a sharp tool and scratch a groove in the edge of the exposed plaster. This will undercut the surface of the plaster and provide a good bedding for the filler. Vacuum or brush out any dust.

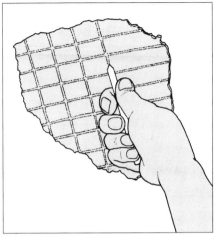

3. With a broad filling knife fill the hole with compound to about ¼ in (6mm) from the surface. When the compound is tacky score some crosshatching with a nail or the edge of the filling knife. Let the filler dry. Apply a second coat of filling compound to within about ⅛ in (3mm) of the surface. Allow to dry.

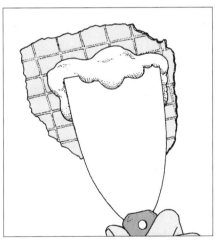

4. Apply the final coat and let it spread 2in (50mm) or so beyond the hole. Sand with fine sandpaper until the surface is smooth to the touch. Seal the repair with a coat of thinned primer-sealer.

LARGE HOLES IN PLASTERBOARD

1. *Outline a square or rectangle around the damaged area and cut it away with a plasterboard saw or jigsaw.*

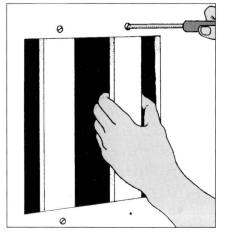

2. *Screw in wooden backing struts.*

3. *Alternatively glue strips of plasterboard behind the hole.*

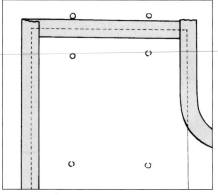

4. *Cut a piece of plasterboard to fill the hole and either screw or glue it to the backing struts. Tape and fill the cracks and fill the screw holes. Sand to a smooth finish and seal with a coat of thinned primer-sealer.*

HOLES IN PLASTERBOARD CEILINGS

This technique will work for holes up to 6in (150mm) wide. A larger hole than that should be repaired with a new piece of plasterboard. Brush away any loose plaster and dampen the edges of the hole. Apply filler to the edges ensuring that some of the compound sticks up into the ceiling cavity.

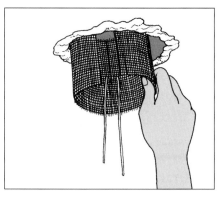

1. *Cut a piece of fine wire mesh about 1in (25mm) larger than the hole. Loop*

string through the centre of the mesh. Roll up the mesh and insert it through the hole. The mesh will open and you will be able to pull it flat across the back of the hole, seating it in the protruding compound.

2. Tie a piece of dowel (a pencil will also do the trick) to the string and turn it until the dowel tightens against the ceiling. Fill the hole with compound until it is about ⅛in (3mm) from the surface. Allow the filler to dry.

3. Cut the string close to the mesh and fill the spot of exposed mesh that remains. Allow the compound to dry. Apply a final coat of filler with a broad knife, allowing the compound to extend a little beyond the hole, thus 'feathering' the filler into the existing plaster. Allow to dry and then rub down with fine sandpaper until the surface is smooth. Seal the repair with a coat of thinned primer-sealer.

REPAIRING 'POPPED' PLASTERBOARD NAILS

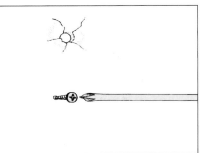

1. Drive a plasterboard screw into the joist 2in (50mm) away from the popped nail. The screw should tighten the plasterboard against the joist.

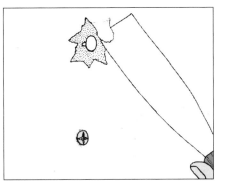

2. Scrape away any loose paint and plaster. Drive the popped nail back into the plasterboard so that its head is sunk below the surface of the board.

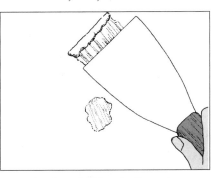

3. With a broad filling knife apply a coat of compound. When dry sand the filler to a smooth finish and seal with a coat of thinned primer-sealer.

PREPARING WOODWORK

Although woodwork is generally the last thing in a room to be painted, it should be prepared at the same time as walls and ceilings.

NEW WOOD

Fill any nail holes and other dents with filling compound. When the compound is dry, lightly sand the whole surface and wipe down with white spirit before applying an all-purpose primer. Once the primer has dried, lightly sand again and wipe off the dust with a cloth and a little white spirit before applying the finishing paint.

Treating knots

Scrape off any hardened resin that has oozed from the knot. Seal the knot with shellac knotting (if you intend to use a light-coloured finishing coat), or an aluminium primer (if you intend to finish with a dark-coloured finishing coat). If you want to finish woodwork with clear varnish or lacquer you will not need to treat knots with shellac. After having sanded the wood to a smooth finish, seal it with a coat of varnish or lacquer.

Wood fillers

If you intend to give woodwork a clear finish choose a wood filler in the appropriate colour to match the wood. Wood fillers (also known as 'stoppers') come in oil or water-based versions. Make sure your filler is compatible with your finishing coat. Some fillers come in ready-mixed paste form, others are sold as paste and separate hardener which need to be mixed. Work the filler well into the wood with a putty knife. When the filler has hardened, rub it down in the direction of the grain.

STAINED WOOD

Lightly sand and prime with an oil-based wood primer. When the primer is dry fill all defects, sand again and dust off debris before applying the finishing paint.

PREVIOUSLY PAINTED WOODWORK

Most previously painted woodwork has been glossed, and new paint will not easily adhere to it. If the surface is in good condition all that need be done is to first lightly sand the surface to roughen it and provide a key for subsequent coatings. Fill all defects, sand again and dust off before applying undercoat.

When the undercoat is dry, sand off lightly to 'de-nib' the surface i.e. rub down any little peaks of hardened paint, brush off and apply the finishing coat.

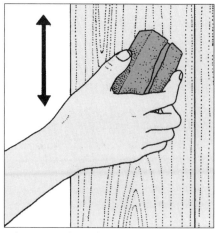

Always work in the direction of the grain.

CHEMICAL STRIPPERS

Check whether you need an alkali-based stripper (for emulsion paint) or spirit-based stripper (for oil-based paint). You can use liquid, gel, or paste ('blanket') forms. The liquid and gel will usually only take off one layer of paint at a time, so they can be quite time-consuming, messy and expensive. Paste is more effective for multi-layered and particularly stubborn paint.

CHEMICAL STRIPPER SAFETY CHECK

1. Chemical strippers are highly corrosive to the skin. Wash thoroughly with soap and water if you get splashed.

2. Wear strong PVC gloves. Protect eyes with goggles if working over your head.

3. Keep the container closed when not in use. Be particularly vigilant if there are children or pets around.

4. Make sure there is adequate ventilation. The toxic fumes from strippers can be harmful. Do not smoke when using strippers.

5. Spirit-based strippers are highly inflammable and should never be used near a naked flame.

6. Protect the surface around the area you are stripping as chemical strippers will damage unprotected paint.

Paste ('blanket') chemical stripper

1. Apply the paste with a narrow filling knife so that it covers the surface thickly, ensuring it is worked into mouldings and crevices.

2. The paste must not be allowed to dry out, so cover it with polythene or the special 'blanket' supplied by the manufacturer. Leave for about five hours or as long as recommended by the manufacturer.

3. The stripper can now be either peeled off (bringing with it the old paint) or scrubbed off with plenty of water and a stiff brush.

Apply a thick layer of paste and leave for about five hours.

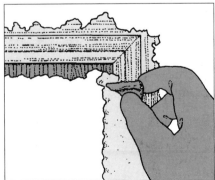

The hardened paste can be peeled off or washed off with water.

Liquid or gel chemical stripper

Brush thickly on to the paintwork, treating smallish areas at a time. Leave for about 20 minutes or until the paint starts to bubble.

Scrape a small area and if the paint is still resistant, brush on another coat of stripper and leave for a further 10 minutes.

1. Brush on the liquid or gel thickly.

2. After about 20 minutes strip off the blistered paint.

3. Scrape the paint with a flat scraper or shavehook.

4. Wash the wood with fine wire wool and white spirit (if using a spirit-based stripper) or water. Always work with the grain, and try not to use too much water as it will swell and raise the grain. Allow the wood to dry thoroughly before sanding and priming.

5. Use fine wire wool and white spirit for final clean-up.

BLEACHING

If stripped wood has become dis-coloured apply a solution of one part household bleach to three parts water (or use a proprietary wood bleach). Allow to dry thoroughly.

HEAT STRIPPING

Using either a gas blowtorch or hot-air gun (electrical or gas-powered) is often the quickest way to strip paint. The blowtorch will be faster than the hot-air gun, but unlike the gun, it involves working with a naked flame with the risk of scorching the wood as well as the greater risk of an accident. Always work from the bottom to the top of the area to be stripped. Heat stripping is hazardous on old lead-based paint as toxic fumes will be given off. If you have any doubts about the old paint, use one of the heat-free stripping techniques described on pages 34-36.

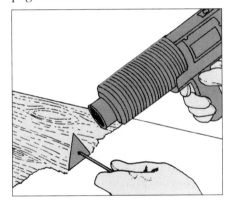

Some hot-air guns use electrically heated air, others gas-heated air. Hold about 4in (100mm) from the surface and scrape while the paint is still bubbling.

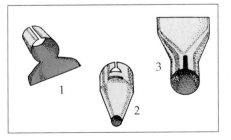

1. For working on glazing bars.
2. For concentrating heat.
3. For spreading heat.

USING A BLOWTORCH

1. Hold the blowtorch 6-8in (150-200mm) from the surface and play it over a small area until the paint bubbles. Scrape flat surfaces with a broad scraper or filling knife.

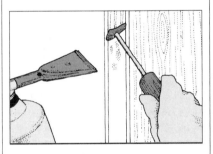

2. Use a shavehook to get into mouldings.

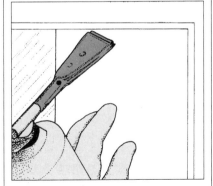

3. Scrape while the paint is still hot. Protect glass with a metal guard, and remember to wear goggles when working above head height.

GUIDELINES FOR HEAT STRIPPING

---

* Do not use a heat stripper if you suspect the paint might have contained lead, as toxic fumes can be given off. This usually only applies to paint over about 10 years old.

* Wear heat-resistant gloves and, if working overhead, goggles and a hat.

* Remove all inflammable material such as curtains, plastic sheet, paper or solvents.

* Take care where the torch or gun is pointing when not being directed at the paint. It is usually while you are concentrating on scraping that accidents happen.

* Never leave an ignited blowtorch or hot-air gun unattended, and take particular care if children are around. Do not let the still hot nozzle of an extinguished torch or gun touch anything inflammable.

* Never leave an area in which you have been using a blowtorch for at least 30 minutes after you have finished. This will give you time to detect any smouldering wood.

* Do not heat-strip dry, rotting wood. It is highly inflammable.

* Put burnt paint into an empty tin or metal bucket, and check that it is not smouldering. Do not allow burnt debris to build up on the floor where it can be a fire hazard.

* Hold the blowtorch or hot-air gun in your least-favoured hand (left hand if you are right-handed and vice versa). Work from right to left if right-handed and left to right if left-handed.

* Work in small areas at a time.

* To avoid scorching with a blowtorch, do not let the flame play on one area for too long. As with hot-air guns, you should aim for a continuous progress over the area to be stripped.

* Do not change a blowtorch cylinder near a naked flame. When the cylinder is punctured there is a small escape of gas (you hear a little hiss).

* Never put your hand in front of a hot-air gun to see if it is working properly.

* Blowtorch flames can easily crack glass. Use a metal shield when working on glazing bars. Hot-air guns do not produce such a fierce heat, but they should be fitted with an appropriate nozzle.

* When working at height with an electric hot-air gun, drape the flex over your shoulder or tape it to the side of the ladder to keep it from entangling your feet.

* If you are working with a hot-air gun powered by a separate gas cylinder, make sure the cylinder is safely supported.

PREPARING METALWORK

If metalwork has a sound gloss surface it need only be roughened for new paint by rubbing down with wet-and-dry paper or fine wire wool abrasives and wiped over with a little white spirit. With bare metal, rub down with wet-and-dry paper or fine wire wool and apply a proprietary rust inhibitor (following the manufacturer's instructions). Wipe with white spirit and a clean cloth to remove any traces of dust. Brush on a zinc-based primer as soon as you can to prevent rust forming. (Rust will form in a few hours on unprotected iron and steel). If, however, you are faced with chipped and flaking paint you will need to remove it:

1. Remove loose paint with a wire brush or the wire-brush attachment of an electric drill (wear goggles and gloves).
2. Brush a proprietary rust inhibitor on to all areas of exposed metal (following the manufacturer's instructions).
3. As soon as the metal is dry, seal it with a zinc-based primer.

ALUMINIUM

Although non-rusting, aluminium can become pitted with corrosion. The following treatment is also suitable for copper piping.

1. Wipe down with white spirit.
2. Rub down with wet-and-dry paper dampened with white spirit (do not use a wire brush or wire wool which will score the surface).
3. Clean off with white spirit and dry the surface with a clean cloth.
4. Seal with a zinc-based primer or, for a clear finish, with polyurethane varnish.

BRASS

Do not use abrasives of any kind because they will scratch the surface. The old lacquer should be removed with a lacquer solvent or white spirit. Wipe over the bare brass with brass polish applied with a soft cloth. Clean off the polish with a little white spirit and, when completely dry, coat the surface with clear lacquer or a polyurethane varnish.

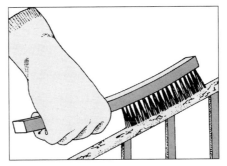

Removing flaking paint on metalwork with a wire brush.

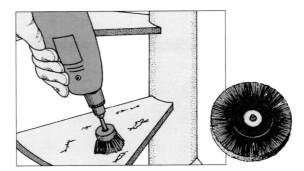

There are various shapes and sizes of wire-brush attachments for an electric drill. Some are designed for covering larger flat areas, while others are shaped to get into awkward corners. Always wear protective goggles and gloves.

GETTING ORGANISED

SEQUENCE OF EVENTS

If you intend doing a complete re-decoration of a room follow the sequence professional decorators use: ceilings first; walls next; woodwork last. Wipe off any paint that falls on to woodwork before it dries – it will save a lot of labour later. If you face a painting and wallpapering job, do the painting first. If the floor is to be painted or sanded, it should be done last of all.

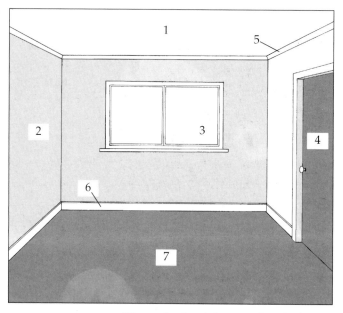

The professional decorator's painting sequence: 1 ceilings, 2 walls, 3 window woodwork, 4 doors, 5 cornices, 6 skirtingboard, 7 floor.

PREPARING PAINT

Paint should always be stirred, even if it has just been purchased, as it may have been on the shelf some time. It is also useful to stir and mix old paint or different batches of the same colour to ensure a uniform finish. Professional decorators will 'box' paint to achieve a thorough mix:

1. If old paint has separated into a thick sediment and thin upper layer, pour off the upper layer into a clean bucket or paint kettle.
2. Stir the thick sediment.
3. Add the thick to the thin, stirring them together.
4. Now pour the paint back and forth between the two containers a few times.

Straining oil paint

Oil-based paints can develop a leathery skin if they have been stored a long time or if the lid has not made an airtight seal. Do not try to stir the skin back into the paint. Cover a clean tin or plastic bucket with old nylon tights or cheesecloth and strain the paint through it.

Paint kettles

It is best not to use paint direct from the manufacturer's tin. Pour the required amount into a paint kettle or small plastic bucket – they are lighter and easier to use. In addition, they will cause less mess if accidentally knocked over.

COVERING SEQUENCE

Start at the top corner of a wall working right to left if right-handed, left to right if left-handed. Work in horizontal bands of 1 sq yd/m sections and keep a wet edge moving across the wall. If you let the paint dry before finishing a whole wall it will leave unsightly stripes of different tones.

SPRAYING

Spraying interior surfaces is really only worthwhile if you have to cover large areas. For most rooms the extra set-up time and the need to carefully mask off any areas not to be painted make spraying much less useful in interiors than exteriors. See pages 153-155 for a full description of techniques. If you do decide to spray indoors make sure there is adequate ventilation.

PAINTING STAIRWELLS

Because stairs are likely to be heavily trafficked, stairwells should be painted last. Particular care should be taken in setting up a safe platform (see page 17).

After repairing plaster or woodwork damage begin by painting the ceiling, followed by the walls (working top to bottom). Finish with the banisters and other woodwork.

PAINTING SKIRTINGBOARD

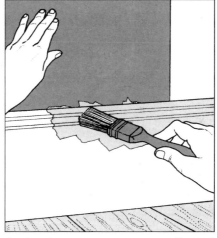

A simple way to protect walls and carpets when painting skirtingboard is to use a piece of stiff card as a paint guard. Alternatively use a metal or plastic shield available from most DIY and paint stockists. Paint the top edge of the board first, then the floor edge.

BASIC BRUSHWORK

1. Hold the brush with the thumb supporting the back.

2. Do not overload the brush with paint. The bristles should be dipped in to about half their length. Touch off some of the excess paint against the inside of the paint kettle which will help prevent the brush becoming overloaded with paint that can drip or run back up the brush handle. Do not draw the brush across the rim.

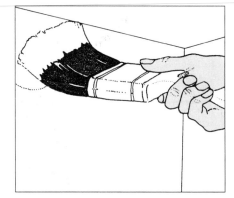

3. Cut in the edges of walls and ceilings, around door frames, over skirtingboard and around switches and light fittings with a 2in (50mm) brush. Use the narrow edge of the brush, pressing enough to flex the bristles. Keep the brush well loaded with paint and watch the paint edge carefully. Use short, smooth strokes.

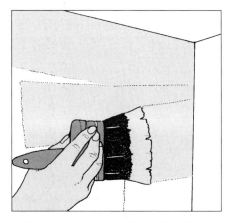

4. Lay the paint on to the wall with a wider brush (4-6in/100-150mm) using long, light strokes. Work the paint in with a criss-cross brush action that will help reduce brush marks. Start at the top corner of the wall working right to left if right-handed, left to right if left-handed. Work in horizontal bands of 1 sq yd/m sections and keep a wet edge moving across the wall.

BASIC ROLLER TECHNIQUES

To remove lint from a new roller sleeve, prime the sleeve with either water (for emulsion and other water-based paint) or white spirit (for oil or alkyd-based paints). Roll the sleeve out on a clean piece of old sheet and leave it to dry for at least 24 hours before painting.

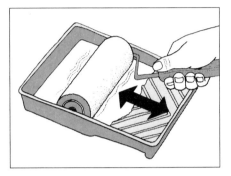

1. *Pour enough paint to fill the trough section of a roller tray. Do not overfill. Put the roller sleeve in the paint and run it up and down the ribbed section a few times until the sleeve is uniformly loaded with paint.*

Walls *After cutting in the edges with a 2in (50mm) brush, start at the top corner and work down the wall. The first rolls should be in a zigzag pattern. Roll upwards on the first stroke to avoid drips. Roll slowly to reduce spraying. Build up a series of diagonal and vertical strokes. Even out the paint with horizontal strokes. When the roller has discharged its paint, lightly roll over the newly painted section using vertical strokes (see step 2 opposite).*

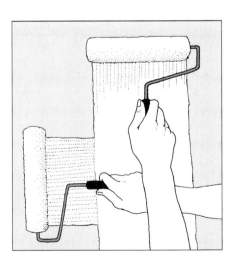

2. *When the roller had discharged its paint, lightly roll over the newly painted section using vertical strokes.*

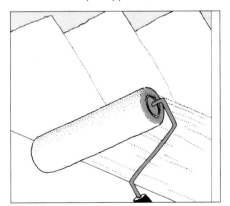

Ceilings *Cut in around the edge of the ceiling with a 2in (50mm) brush. Roll diagonally in 1 sq yd/m sections. Go over the diagonal strokes rolling parallel to the wall and get in as closely as you can to the edge. To finish off a section cover the area by rolling lightly with an unloaded roller.*

APPLYING TEXTURED PAINT

Apart from aesthetic considerations, textured paint is very useful for covering less-than-perfect surfaces (although cracks of more than ⅛in/3mm width will have to be filled). New surfaces need only have serious defects repaired. Wallpaper should be stripped and walls should be sound, clean and dry. Gloss finishes should be sanded. Check that old lathe-and-plaster ceilings can take the extra weight.

Use either a wide ('distemper') brush of 7-8in (175-200mm) or a foam-rubber-sleeved roller. In addition, you can buy roller sleeves specially designed to give different effects. As you will be putting on only one coat, apply the paint thickly.

Textured paint dries in 12 to 24 hours and can form sharp peaks and knobs that should be sanded down. With some textured paint it may be necessary to go over it with a coat or two of regular paint.

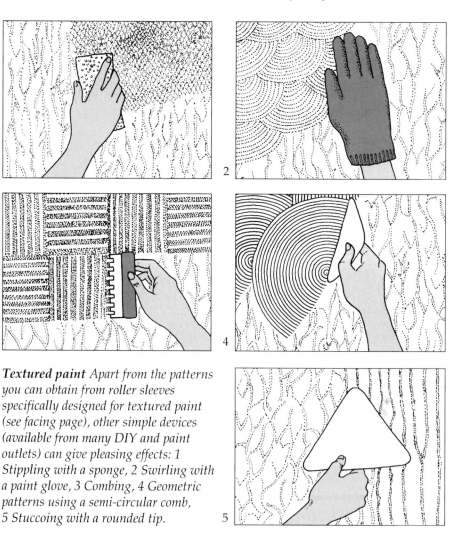

Textured paint Apart from the patterns you can obtain from roller sleeves specifically designed for textured paint (see facing page), other simple devices (available from many DIY and paint outlets) can give pleasing effects: 1 Stippling with a sponge, 2 Swirling with a paint glove, 3 Combing, 4 Geometric patterns using a semi-circular comb, 5 Stuccoing with a rounded tip.

There are many kinds of paint roller sleeves available specifically designed for textured paint.

DOORS

* Doors should be painted after ceilings and walls but before skirting-boards.

* Remove all handles and other hardware and make sure all surfaces are clean and free of dust (do not forget the top edge).

* Make repairs and prepare as described on page 34-38.

* Aim to finish the whole door in one session to avoid texture and colour problems that can arise if you let part of the job dry.

* Use one coat of undercoat over a light colour, two to obliterate a dark colour.

* For finishing coats use a 1in (25mm) brush for mouldings and a 2in (50mm) brush for the larger flat areas.

* Lay on the paint in the direction of the grain and work it in with a criss-cross brush action to even out the paint. Finish off by brushing lightly in the direction of the grain to eliminate brush marks.

FLUSH DOORS

Start at the top and work down in sections of 9-12in (225-300mm) square. Lay on paint with a criss-cross action, spreading the paint out in order to avoid runs. Lay the paint off with light vertical brush strokes which eliminate brush marks. To avoid paint runs make sure you do not put too much paint on the top sections.

Painting sequence for panel doors
Professional painters and decorators tackle a panel door in strict sequence:
1. Mouldings
2. Inside of panels
3. Centre rails
4. Top and bottom rails
5. Stiles
6. Top, hinge and front edges
7. Frame

WINDOWS

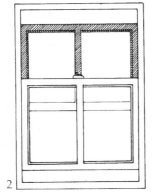

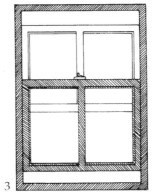

Painting sequence for sash windows

1. Lower the inner (top) sash and raise the outer (bottom) sash. Paint the bottom rail and as much of the side rail of the outer sash as possible.

2. Reverse the positions of the sashes and finish the inner sash.

3. Paint the outer sash, frame and inside runners (the grooves in which the sashes slide).

4. Make sure the sashes can move before the paint in the runners has dried completely.

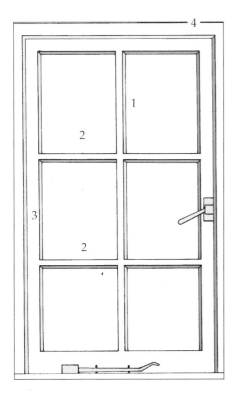

Painting sequence for casement windows *Take off all hardware if possible. Tack a nail into the underside of the window to act as a temporary handle. With the window open, paint the glazing bars (1 and 2). Now paint the horizontal and vertical rails (3) followed by the frame (4).*

KEEPING PAINT OFF THE GLASS

Use a cutting-in brush (see page 22) and protect the glass either by using

(a) masking tape around the edge of the glazing bars and rails (remember to peel off the tape before the paint has completely dried or you might take off paint from the woodwork) or (b) a plastic or metal paint shield (see page 21).

If paint does dry on the glass it can be scraped off with a razor-blade knife (available from most DIY and paint stockists).

CLEANING UP

Brushes and roller sleeves used with emulsion or other water-based paints are easy to clean. Simply wash them out in clean water to which a little washing-up liquid has been added. Rinse in clean water and allow to dry. If you have been using oil or alkyd-based paints follow these steps:

BRUSHES

1. Remove excess paint by scraping the bristles against the edge of a piece of board.
2. Pour sufficient white spirit into a clean tin or jar to cover the bristles and come half way up the metal band (ferrule) of the brush. Work the spirit into the bristles and change the spirit until it is no longer being discoloured by paint. Shake off excess spirit on the cloth or newspaper. Or, better still, spin the brush inside a cardboard box.
3. Using a comb (available from most DIY and paint suppliers) or wire brush, tease out any remaining particles of paint that may be lodged in the bristles.
4. Rinse out the brush in a solution of warm water and detergent to remove all traces of white spirit.
5. Rinse in clean water.
6. Remove any excess water by spinning the brush. Smooth the bristles back into shape and leave the brush to dry, hanging by its handle.
7. When the brush is dry wrap the bristles in brown paper or aluminium foil (see diagram) and store it flat or hanging by the handle.

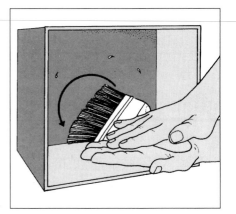

Spinning a brush inside a cardboard box is a good way to get rid of excess white spirit during cleaning.

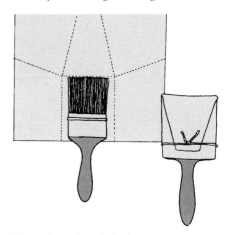

Wrapping a brush for long-term storage.

ROLLERS

1. Roll out as much paint as you can onto newspaper.
2. Remove the sleeve and soak it in white spirit.
3. Wearing rubber gloves squeeze out as much of the white spirit as you can and, when the nap is dry, wrap it in brown paper or plastic wrap.
4. Store standing on one end to prevent flattening the nap.

RESTORING BRUSHES

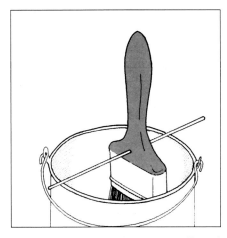

If the bristles have become stiffened with dry paint, drill a hole through the base of the handle and suspend the bristles and a good part of the ferrule in paraffin, white spirit or a proprietary brush restoring solvent.

Once the bristles are loosened comb out any remaining paint particles. Wash the bristles thoroughly in soapy water to which a little white spirit has been added. Rinse in clean water and allow to dry.

STORING PAINT

Keep paints and solvents in a dry, cool place but protected from frost. Keep them locked away or on a shelf high enough to be out of the reach of children.

Cut a circle of wax paper large enough to cover the whole surface of the paint. Float the paper lid on the paint to keep air out. Clear the channel in the rim of the tin of any paint and ensure the lid fits tightly. Label tins with the date, colour reference and room in which it was used.

DISPOSAL

Solvents and thinners that have become discoloured with paint should not be poured down the drain or put in a dustbin. Call your local authority's environmental officer for specific advice about disposal facilities in your area.

SHORT-TERM STORAGE

If you do not want to laboriously clean your brushes and roller sleeves at the end of each day's work for use next morning, suspend brushes in white spirit or water (whichever is appropriate for the paint you have been working with) as described in 'Restoring brushes' on this page. Roller sleeves can be immersed in water or white spirit poured into a foil baking tin. Before you resume painting make sure you shake or roll out all traces of water or spirit.

If you need to leave your brush or roller for an hour or so, wrap it in clingfilm to prevent air getting to the paint.

SPECIAL PAINT TECHNIQUES

Special paint techniques (sometimes described as 'broken colour' or 'distressing') offer an exciting and economical alternative to straightforward painting or wallpapering.

Although some techniques, such as advanced marbling and wood graining, require specialist skills; those included here are well within the capacity of most DIY painters and decorators.

Special paint techniques fall into two basic categories: those that involve applying the finishing glaze over the dried base coat (e.g. sponging-on, ragging-on, and colour-washing) and those that involve removing some of the finishing glaze while it is still wet (e.g. sponging-off and ragging-off, stippling, combing). In each case, though, the aim is the same – to 'distress' the surface glaze and allow the base coat to show through.

The rich decorative possibilities opened up by special paint techniques can sometimes lead to visual overkill. It is not necessary to smother every available surface in stipple or stencil. Marbling, for example, should be used on those surfaces that might reasonably have been made of marble: walls and floors, for example, rather than doors or window frames.

SURFACE	RECOMMENDED TECHNIQUES
New plaster (dried for at least 6 months, primed)	all
Rough plaster (cracks filled, rubbed down, primed)	sponging, ragging, colour-washing, stencilling
New woodwork (filled, rubbed down, primed)	dragging, stencilling, stippling, marbling, rag-rolling, ragging, sponging
Painted woodwork (rubbed down, filled, primed)	sponging, ragging, marbling stencilling
Metal (rubbed down, primed)	all
Lining paper (over smooth surface, sealed)	all
Concrete (smooth, primed)	ragging, sponging, colour-washing, stencilling
Stone/brickwork (sealed)	sponging, colour-washing, ragging

Left:: *Hardboard tiles have been marbled to give this severely-proportioned bathroom some softening colours, patterning and texture. For marbling techniques, see pages 72–75.* Above: *The realistic-looking marble effect has been painted using the techniques described on pages 72–75. The restrained colours accentuate the formality of the room.*

TOOLS AND PREPARATION

Essentially, walls and woodwork need to be prepared as for conventional painting (see pages 28–38). Some special paint techniques such as sponging, stippling and ragging are particularly useful in helping to hide irregularities because the illusion of texture they create diverts the eye.

Walls covered with non-textured wallpaper that is sound need not be stripped. Stick back any loose seams or edges and seal with a coat of primer-sealer if the pattern is strongly coloured. Vinyl-coated paper will have to be stripped to its backing and, if sound, the backing paper will have to be sealed with a couple of coats of thinned emulsion.

It is not necessary to prepare walls with an oil-based paint when using oil glaze, in fact it would be tedious and impractical over a large area. All woodwork should be brought up to an eggshell (i.e. oil-based) finish but walls can be coated with a vinyl-silk emulsion. If you intend to use an oil glaze, an eggshell base

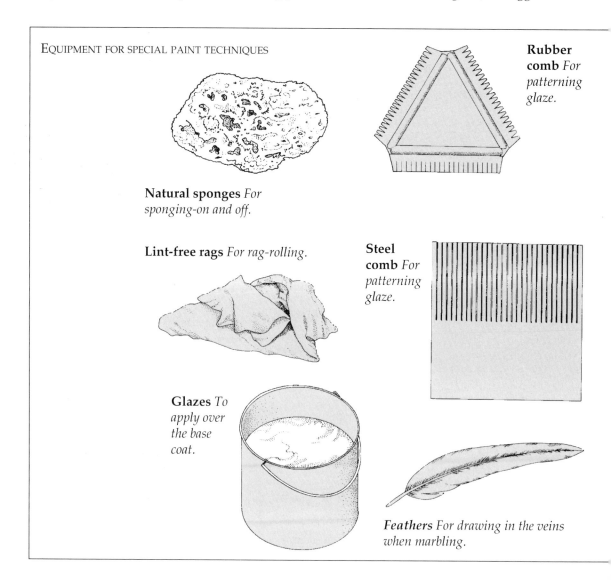

EQUIPMENT FOR SPECIAL PAINT TECHNIQUES

Rubber comb *For patterning glaze.*

Natural sponges *For sponging-on and off.*

Lint-free rags *For rag-rolling.*

Steel comb *For patterning glaze.*

Glazes *To apply over the base coat.*

Feathers **Feathers** *For drawing in the veins when marbling.*

paint is probably the best. It is important, however, that the paint is brushed on using criss-cross strokes to eradicate brush marks and achieve a really smooth finish. Rolling can never achieve the same degree of smoothness.

If the wall has been repaired and filled, seal the new patches with primer-sealer before painting with the base coat or the filled areas will absorb the base coat.

Embossed paper need not be stripped. If it is wiped with glaze it will give an extra dimension to the effect.

Before you start it is a good idea to experi-ment on a piece of coated hardboard until you get just the right combination of base coat and finishing glaze colours.

Most special effect techniques start with a base coat in white or cream, over which the finishing glaze is applied once the base coat is completely dry. However, very pleas-ing effects can be achieved by using different-coloured base coats and experimenting with lighter or darker-coloured glazes of a com-plementary hue to the base coat, e.g. a rose-pink base coat with a light pink glaze, or *vice versa.*

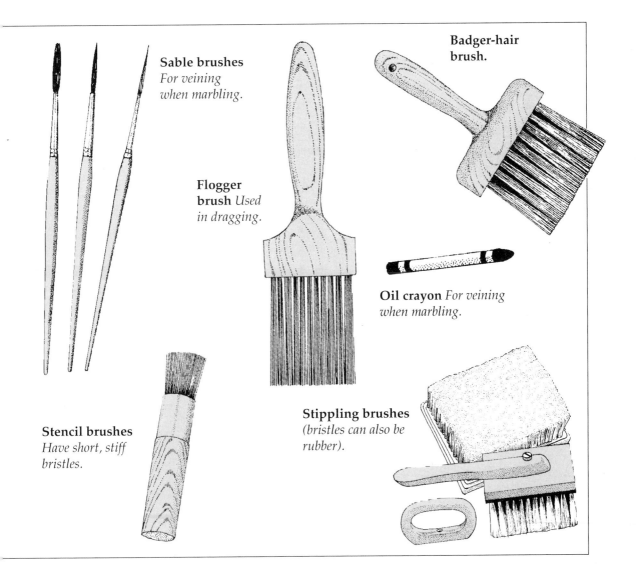

Sable brushes *For veining when marbling.*

Badger-hair brush.

Flogger brush *Used in dragging.*

Oil crayon *For veining when marbling.*

Stencil brushes *Have short, stiff bristles.*

Stippling brushes *(bristles can also be rubber).*

Opposite: *The walls of this cheerful dining room have been sponged (see pages 60–62). When the sponging had dried a small flower-motif stencil was randomly dotted over the wall to emphasise the summery theme. For stencil techniques see pages 68–72.*

Above: *The walls have been simply sponged (see pages 60–62) – a relatively quick and uncomplicated special paint technique that softens and adds texture to the overall scheme of the room.*

Left: *A child's room brightened with multi-coloured stencils. For stencilling in more than one colour see pages 68–72.*

GLAZE

FINISH GUIDE		
Finish	Glaze	Suitability
COLOUR-WASHING	Emulsion	Very good results. Most people prefer this finish
	Oil glaze	Good
	Paint glaze	Good
MARBLING	Emulsion	Good
	Oil glaze	Good
	Paint glaze	Good
SPONGING-ON	Emulsion	Good
	Oil glaze	Good, result is crisper
	Paint glaze	Good
SPONGING-OFF	Emulsion	Not suitable
	Oil glaze	Good
	Paint glaze	Difficult at best
STIPPLING	Emulsion	Not suitable
	Oil glaze	Good
	Paint glaze	Difficult on large areas
DRAGGING	Emulsion	Not suitable
	Oil glaze	Good
	Paint glaze	Difficult on large areas
RAGGING-ON	Emulsion	Good
	Oil glaze	Good
	Paint glaze	Good
RAGGING-OFF	Emulsion	Not suitable
	Oil glaze	Good
	Paint glaze	Difficult on large areas

*For emulsion glaze use an emulsion base coat; for oil glaze a vinyl silk or eggshell base coat; for paint glaze (using oil paint) use a vinyl silk or eggshell base coat.

To achieve the most luminous effect, most professionals use a transparent oil glaze (sometimes called 'scumble glaze') tinted with artists' oil and then thinned 1:1 with white spirit.

There are many different manufacturers of scumble and they may recommend different thinning proportions. For example, one of the leading manufacturers recommends an addition of one part white spirit to four parts scumble. Take care not to overthin the scumble or you might cause the pigment to separate.

If you want to lighten the glaze colour and soften the overall effect add white oil-based undercoat (thinned with white spirit to the consistency of single cream) a tablespoon at a time to the glaze. Mix it well until you achieve the shade you want.

Small amounts of acid-refined linseed oil (about five tablespoons to a litre of glaze) will slow down the drying time of the glaze, which is particularly useful when working on a large area.

An alternative to the colour-mixing process is to find an oil-based paint in the colour you want and thin it with an equal amount of white spirit. The simplest glaze of all is made with emulsion thinned three or four parts water to one part paint.

Although transparent oil glaze is probably the smelliest option it does stay wet much longer than the other two types of glaze thus giving you more time to distress it. This is useful because at all costs you need to avoid the job drying out before it is finished as the hard line of the dried edge will be extremely difficult to disguise later.

Mix sufficient glaze to finish the

COLOUR-WASHING

job, not only do you need to avoid the drying problem but it is also very difficult to mix later batches to match the colour of the first. As a rule of thumb, thinned oil glaze will cover 20-40 sq m per litre.

Do not use oil glaze on radiators or hot pipes as heat tends to yellow it, as does lack of sunlight (for example, the glaze behind a picture will yellow much more quickly than glaze in direct sunlight). Yellowing can be minimised by adding a little white undercoat to the glaze.

MIXING GLAZES

Squeeze a little of the artist's oil paint into a clean container such as a jam jar and dissolve the paint in a little white spirit. Add some of the paint to the transparent glaze, stirring continuously – adding more paint if necessary – until you have the colour you want. Now dilute the glaze with about an equal quantity of white spirit (or follow the manufacturer's instructions). A little acid-refined linseed oil can also be added to retard the drying time of the glaze.

A white emulsion base coat can be tinted with artists' gouache or acrylic paint dissolved in a little water, added to the base coat and stirred until the correct shade is achieved. It is then thinned with three to four times as much water as paint. Test a little of the glaze on the surface you wish to cover. It will look darker in the container than it does on the wall. Water-soluble glazes should be protected, when dry, with a coat of acrylic varnish or a proprietary varnish formulated especially for emulsion paint.

By applying a coat, or a series of coats, of thinned, almost translucent, paint over a base coat the underlying colour is softened and warmed. In effect, the wash acts as a colour filter.

Washes can be made from thinned oil or water-based paints, although the technique is used mainly with water-based washes.

For a very translucent wash add about two tablespoons of white emulsion tinted with artists' gouache or acrylic colour to one litre of water. Add a small amount of white emulsion to the water to give the wash enough body to adhere to the surface. Add one teaspoon of PVA to one litre of wash for durability.

Undercoat the wall with a water-based paint. Using a wide brush, paint the wash on to the wall with broad, flowing strokes. Keep a sponge or soft brush in the other hand for working drips back into the surface. Leave the first wash coat to dry thoroughly before applying further coats (allowing each to dry before adding another) until you achieve the density of colour you want. If the surface is in a much used part of the house it is advisable to seal the wash with acrylic varnish.

Washes can also be made with oil-based or vinyl silk undercoat, tinted with artist's oils and thinned with an equal amount of white spirit to undercoat. This wash should be brushed on to a wall undercoated with an oil-based paint. Make sure the surface is free of grease by washing it down with a cloth dampened with white spirit. A matt polyurethane varnish (applied after the wash has dried) will protect the surface.

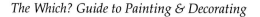

Above: *The walls here have been stippled in grey to soften the clean lines of the rest of the decor. For stippling technique see pages 61 and 63.*

Right: *Special paint techniques such as rag-rolling (see pages 65 and 67) can be used to cover larger areas of wall with broad drifts of colour.*

SPONGING

Sponging is one of the easiest of the special techniques. It offers a great variety of effects depending on the interplay of the colours of the base and glaze coats; on whether the glaze is matt or glossy; on the pressure with which the glaze is applied, or on whether glaze coats in different colours are applied.

Sponging produces a busy pattern that is particularly useful in helping to camouflage irregular surfaces.

Variety of pattern also comes from the nature of the sponge itself. Although sea sponges are expensive, their unique construction gives a variety to the patterning that is impossible to duplicate with an artificial sponge. If you have to use an artificial sponge, however, cut it in a random way with a Stanley knife to approximate the irregularity of a natural sponge.

Prepare a new sponge by soaking it in an appropriate solvent (water for water-based glaze; white spirit for oil glaze), wring it out and use it when only slightly damp.

There are two ways of sponging. The first, and perhaps easiest, is to remove wet glaze (that has been brushed over a dry base coat) with a clean sponge ('sponging-off'). The second involves applying wet glaze with the sponge to the dried base coat ('sponging-on'). Sponging is a good method of covering relatively large areas of wall with a water-based glaze (over a vinyl silk or egg-shell base coat) because a big sponge will cover large areas quickly, and there is less concern about the glaze drying out too quickly. If you want the crisper definition of oil glaze then sponging-off may be the best solution. The problem with sponging-off using a water-based glaze is that the glaze dries more rapidly than its oil counterpart and so cuts down the time for sponging. Of course, two people working in tandem makes for a much easier job.

Whichever glaze you use, ensure that it is quite thin (as a rule of thumb, four parts water to one part emulsion or just over one part white spirit to one part oil glaze). If you are working in warm conditions with a water-based glaze retard the drying time by first sponging the surface with a little water.

SPONGING-OFF

1. Ensure the base coat is thoroughly dry (it should be of vinyl silk or eggshell for a water-based glaze, and oil-based for an oil glaze).
2. Using a broad brush, apply the glaze with cross-hatch strokes in a vertical strip about 3ft (1m) wide.
3. Soak a clean sponge in the appropriate solvent (water or white spirit) and squeeze it out thoroughly. The more solvent that remains in the sponge, the more glaze will be removed and the lighter the end result.
4. Pat the sponge on to the glaze, making sure it hits the surface squarely without skidding.
5. When you lift off the sponge after each pat, turn it slightly in order to vary the pattern. Try to avoid repetition of patterning.
6. As the sponge becomes loaded with glaze, rinse it out and change the solvent when it becomes too discoloured.
7. If you use a water-based glaze you may want to protect the surface with

STIPPLING

a coat of acrylic varnish, brushed on when the glaze is completely dry. An oil-based glaze can be protected with a matt polyurethane varnish if necessary.

SPONGING-ON

If you want to apply coats of different-coloured glaze (applying each only when the previous coat is completely dry) sponging-on is probably easier than sponging-off.

1. When the base coat has thoroughly dried, pour some glaze into the well of a roller tray.

2. Dip the sponge into the glaze and press out any excess on the ribbed part of the tray. Do not overload the sponge or you will be continually mopping up runs or creating ugly over-glazed prints.

3. Make relatively light pats on to the surface. Again, try to strike the surface squarely in order not to skid and smear the glaze.

4. Reposition the sponge for each dab to create a more varied pattern.

5. A large sponge will have difficulty getting into corners. Use a small piece of sponge or paint in dots with a fine artist's brush to simulate sponge marks.

6. The sponge may eventually become clogged with glaze, thus blurring the definition of the pattern. Occasionally rinse it in the appropriate solvent and ring it out thoroughly. It is best, though, to try to complete a whole surface without rinsing the sponge. A rinsed sponge will, at first, tend to dilute and lighten the glaze.

7. If you want to lighten the effect, go over it with a sponge of white paint, as shown on page 62.

The aim is to remove fine points of wet glaze with the bristle tips of a stippling or other stiff-bristled brush to reveal the colour of the base coat. The best effects are achieved with light-coloured glazes stippled over a dark-coloured base coat.

Stippling brushes can be expensive and an alternative is to use a stiff-bristled clothes- or shoe-brush. A long-napped roller will also create a stippled effect.

1. When stippling a wall, brush a strip of glaze (making sure the base coat is thoroughly dry) about 3ft (1m) wide from ceiling to floor. Starting at the top, strike the glaze lightly with the bristle ends of the stippling brush, making sure they strike the glaze square on so as to avoid skidding and smearing the glaze. The process can be greatly speeded up if one person lays on the strips of glaze while another stipples.

2. Continue the strips across the wall, ensuring you complete the whole wall without letting individual strips dry out.

3. Stipple across the joins between strips for continuity of finish.

4. As the stippling brush becomes overloaded with glaze wipe the bristles off on a lint-free rag.

5. If a small area is missed, brush a little glaze on to the stippling brush and dab it on to the wall rather than trying to paint glaze directly on to the wall and then stippling it off.

SPONGING-ON

1. The natural sponge has been dipped in glaze and then squeezed so that it does not hold too much paint. The sponge is then lightly dabbed over the wall. Turn the sponge slightly between dabs in order to vary the pattern.

2. A second sponge can be used to dab on white paint if you want to soften the first sponged colour.

SPONGING-OFF

1. Brush on the glaze (over the dried base coat) in broad cross-hatch strokes. Work in vertical strips about 3ft (1m) wide.

2. Use a clean natural sponge impregnated with solvent to dab off the wet glaze. Turn the sponge often to vary the pattern and avoid letting the sponge skid over the wet glaze.

STIPPLING

1. *Brush on broad swathes and swirls of glaze.*

2. *Use a stippling brush (see page 53) to remove some of the glaze. Do not let the brush slide over the glaze. Use short, light dabbing strokes that do not hit the surface so hard that they splay the bristles.*

DRAGGING

Dragging is a type of simple wood-graining technique which, if done skilfully, can give a silky look to woodwork and walls. Essentially, a dry brush is pulled – 'dragged' – through fresh wet glaze (on large areas such as walls scumble glaze is best for beginners because it takes longer to dry) leaving the slightly irregular lines of the bristle tracks as pattern. It is best to drag on a smooth surface because, unlike other special paint techniques such as sponging or stippling, the straight lines will show up any surface irregularities.

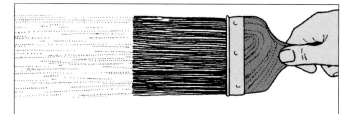

When dragging, do not hold the brush too tightly.

DRAGGING WALLS

Dragging a large area of wall is best done by two people: one to brush or roller on the glaze in 3ft (1m) vertical strips; the other to drag. It is important to drag before the glaze has become sticky and unyielding.

1. Once the base coat is thoroughly dry, roller or brush a vertical strip of glaze 3ft (1m) wide.
2. Starting at the top left-hand corner (if right-handed; top right-hand corner if left-handed), pull a wide, dry paint brush down through the glaze in an uninterrupted line. Put enough pressure on the brush to slightly flex the bristles. Do not hold the brush too tightly; it is easier to get straight lines if the brush is held lightly, thus reducing shake.
3. If you cannot complete the pass

right to the bottom of the wall, stop a few inches from the bottom and drag the brush up from the bottom until it meets the existing tracks.
4. Wipe excess glaze from the brush on to a lint-free cloth after each pass.
5. On subsequent passes, overlap the previous pass to avoid either the build up of dried glaze edges or gaps between passes.

DRAGGING DOORS

1. When the base coat is dry, brush on the glaze using a clean dragging brush (a 2in/50mm paint brush is best for stiles (uprights) and rails (cross-members). A decorator's paper-hanging brush is best for the panels).
2. On panelled doors (see diagram page 65), drag the mouldings first, followed by the panels and then the stiles and rails. Drag in the same direction as the grain: vertically on stiles and horizontally on rails.
3. When dragging down, remove the brush before you reach the bottom of the pass and then turn the brush and drag up from the bottom. This will prevent the build-up of glaze at the bottom of the door.
4. Wipe excess glaze from the brush on a lint-free rag after each pass.

RAGGING

Like sponging, ragging can be either an additive ('ragging-on') or sub-tractive ('ragging-off') technique. Ragging-on works well with any type of glaze, although ragging-off is best with oil (scumble) glaze. Thinned eggshell is also suitable for ragging-off if you add a little raw linseed oil to retard the drying time

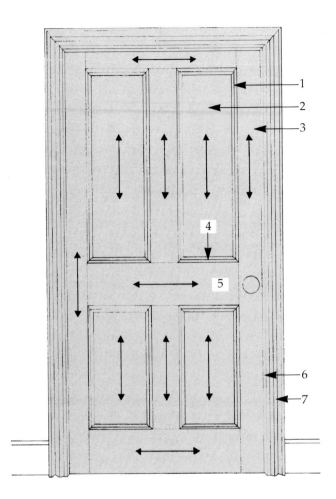

Sequence and directions for dragging a door.

2. Hold the rag lightly and dab it on the surface without squeezing out the glaze.
3. Between dabs, re-bunch the rag or turn it slightly to give variations of pattern.
4. On a wall, work across a 3ft (lm) strip, from top to bottom, soaking and wringing out the rag periodically.

RAGGING-OFF

1. Once the base coat is dry, brush or roller on the glaze in a 3ft (lm) vertical strip. Roller or brush vertically and horizontally to achieve a solid coat of glaze.
2. Soak a lint-free rag in white spirit and wring it out thoroughly. If you are using oil (scumble) glaze, the rag does not need to be soaked in white spirit unless you find that the glaze is not being lifted off easily.
3. Bunch the rag as for ragging-on and dab off the glaze, moving across the strip from top to bottom. As with ragging-off, avoid skidding and vary the orientation of the rag for variety of pattern.
4. If the rag becomes soaked with glaze ring it out periodically, but try to avoid rinsing it in solvent until a whole surface is finished, as a newly rinsed rag will dilute and lighten the glaze compared to the previously ragged-off area.

RAG-ROLLING

Essentially rag-rolling involves the same techniques as ragging-on or off. The difference is that the rag is rolled into a cylinder or sausage shape rather than bunched into a ball. It is rolled over the surface rather than dabbed, and tends to give a pattern with more movement than a dabbed rag.

of the glaze. Ragging-off is certainly much easier if two people are involved: one applying the glaze, the other ragging-off.

RAGGING-ON

1. Once the base coat is dry, take a lint-free rag and soak it in glaze. Ring out the rag and bunch into an irregular-shaped ball.

SAFETY NOTE

Rags that have been soaked in white spirit, oil glaze or oil paint can be dangerously combustible if left bunched up in a pile. Lay them flat (or draped over the rungs of a ladder, for example) to allow the volatile spirits to evaporate. When the rags are completely dry dispose of them, preferably in a metal bin with a lid.

DRAGGING A DOOR

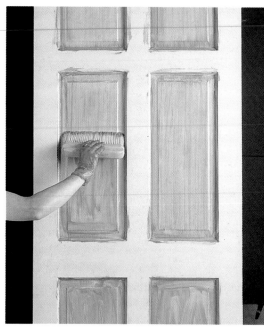

1. Use a paperhanger's brush to drag the glaze down the panels in the direction of the grain.

2. With a narrower brush drag down the joins between panel, stile (the vertical bars of a door) and rails (horizontal bars).

3. Switching back to the broad brush, drag down the stiles.

4. Finish the door by dragging across the rails.

RAGGING-ON

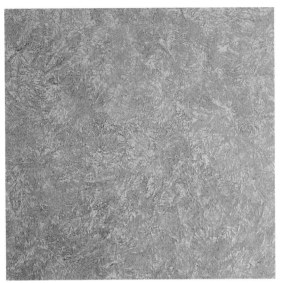

1. When the base coat has dried use bunched lint-free rag with which to dab on the glaze. Turn the rag often and re-bunch it periodically to give some variety of pattern.

2. The finished effect: a pattern that is fairly tight and free-form.

RAG-ROLLING-ON

RAG-ROLLING-OFF

In place of the bunched rag used in ragging-on, roll up the rag into a cylinder shape and apply the glaze. Continually change the direction in which you roll in order to ensure a varied pattern.

Brush on swathes of glaze, and while it is wet use a clean lint-free rag rolled into a cylinder shape to remove areas of glaze. Continually change the direction of your rolling in order to vary the pattern.

STENCILLING

In recent years stencilling has become one of the most popular decorative paint techniques. It is relatively easy to execute, although care has to be taken (especially if working in more than one colour) to get the best result.

STENCILS

Many art materials shops as well as DIY and painting and decorating stockists keep pre-cut stencils, but it is great fun to make your own.
1. Buy either traditional waxed stencil board or acetate sheet (acetate has the advantage of allowing you to see through the stencil to the surface – handy when stencilling in more than one colour and need to align a different stencil for each colour).
2. Either trace a pattern on to tracing paper or photocopy it. Patterns can be enlarged easily on a photocopier or you can scale up a pattern by using gridded paper.
3. If using tracing paper and stencil board, put a piece of carbon paper inked side down on to the board. Put the tracing paper over the carbon paper and trace off the pattern using a pencil or knitting needle. If using a photocopied pattern, spray the back with spray adhesive (available in art supply shops) and stick it to the board or acetate.
4. Put the board or acetate on to a cutting surface (chipboard is fine) and, using a Stanley knife for the bigger cuts and a scalpel (available from art supply shops) for the finer detail, cut out the pattern. Cut towards you and rotate the board as necessary rather than leaning over the board at an awkward angle. Remember, knives and scalpels

should never be left unattended if there are children around.

MULTICOLOUR STENCILS

If you are using stencil board:
1. Trace your pattern on to paper.
2. Using felt-tip pens, shade in the different colour areas.
3. Transfer the outline for each colour area on to separate boards.
4. Cut out the outline on each board.
5. Stack the boards until the whole pattern aligns and, keeping the pattern aligned, trim all the boards to the same size.
6. With the pattern aligned, cut V-shaped notches through the centre of the edges of all the boards. These notches will sit on the guideline of the surface to be stencilled.

If using acetate sheet, draw dotted registration marks on each stencil to indicate the exact positions the other stencils will occupy. See illustration on facing page and page 71.

PAINT

Every type of paint can be used, but a good rule is to use compatible base and stencil coats. On an emulsioned wall use a water-based stencil paint (poster paint, acrylic, gouache, diluted with a little water) or simply another emulsion. On oil-based surfaces use artists' oils diluted with a little white spirit. Cellulose-based spray paints such as those used on car body repairs are ideal for stencilling on metal and walls, but make sure though that the surface has been sealed with shellac and that the surrounding area has been masked-off.

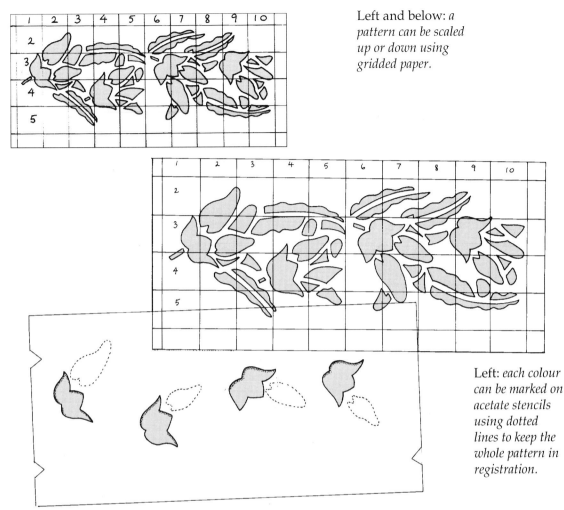

Left and below: *a pattern can be scaled up or down using gridded paper.*

Left: *each colour can be marked on acetate stencils using dotted lines to keep the whole pattern in registration.*

The consistency of stencil paint should be creamy. If it is too wet it will run under the stencil.

PREPARING THE SURFACE

Make sure the surface is clean, dry and dust free. Using a spirit level and a straightedge mark a horizontal guideline with white chalk or very faint pencil. The registration notches on the sides of the stencils will sit on this line.

Plan the work carefully, dividing the distance to be covered along each wall by the width of the stencil. You will almost certainly have to adjust spacing between stencil repeats, and professionals favour working from opposite corners towards the centre. Offer up the stencil and align the notches on the line and secure it with 'low tack' masking tape (other types of tape might mark the wall).

Alternatively, fix the stencil with artists' spray adhesive which is naturally low tack and easy to use. Spray it on to the back of the stencil and allow it to dry for a minute or two before sticking the stencil to the surface. Repositioning the stencil is easy as the spray adhesive stays tacky for some time. At the end of the job clean the back of the stencil with white spirit.

STENCILLING

1. The surface should be clean, dry and dust-free, Use a spirit-level to mark a horizontal guideline. The registration marks on the stencils will sit on this guideline.

2. The stencils can be held up to the wall but it will probably be easier to spray the back of the stencil with spray adhesive. When applying the paint or glaze use short stabbing strokes in order to avoid the paint or glaze spreading under the stencil. If you intend to use more than one colour, complete the whole run of the pattern in the first colour and let it dry before applying subsequent colours.

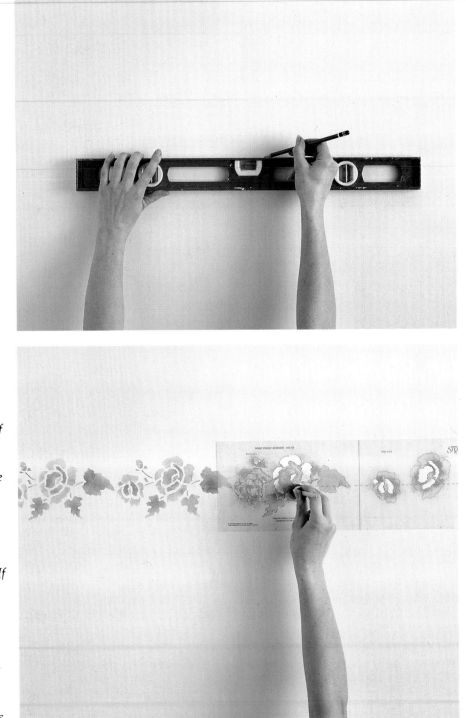

3. *Acetate sheet is easier to use than stencil board when working in multicolours because the previous colours and pattern are easy to see through the acetate. Registration marks are lined up with the horizontal guideline and the second colour is applied with a stubby stencil brush.*
Below: *Completed stencilling.*

STENCILLING TECHNIQUE

* Do not overload the brush with paint to avoid paint runs creeping under the stencil. Similarly, if using a spray paint, do not overspray.
* Keep the stencil flat to the wall by holding it with the rubber tip of a pencil, for example. Alternatively you can spray the back of the stencil with spray adhesive which allows you to lift and stick repeatedly.
* Use short, stabbing strokes but do not apply so much pressure that the bristles will spread under the stencil.
* If the edges of the stencil cut-outs become clogged with paint wipe them periodically and make sure the backs are free of paint before putting them back on the surface.
* When stencilling in more than one colour, complete whole runs in one colour at a time and allow it to dry out completely before applying any further colours.
* Protect the stencil pattern with matt polyurethane varnish (except in the case of matt emulsion, which will tend to suck in polyurethane varnish and darken the colour of the stencil pattern. Use acrylic varnish in this case).

The dark areas on each acetate sheet represent a cut-out for a different colour. The dotted areas are registration guides for the whole pattern, the notches will sit on the guideline of the surface to be stencilled and keep the pattern aligned. Each sheet is identified in the top corner.

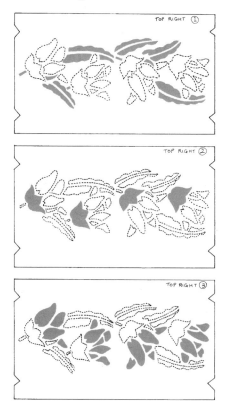

MARBLING

Marbling is one of the oldest decorative painting techniques and in the hands of professionals has been elevated almost to a minor art form. There are hundreds, if not thousands, of different types of marble, and it is not possible, within the scope of this book, to give anything other than basic ground rules to get the DIY painter started.

Marbling can be very realistic, but remember that it is an overall effect you are after rather than a slavish imitation. Certainly, at first, that effect might be a little crude, with more folksy appeal than pretentiousness, but in most domestic settings a freer patterning is more appropriate.

Marble only those things that might logically have been made of marble: mantlepieces rather than window frames; floors and skirting-board rather than doors. Because marble is most commonly sold in slabs about 4 x 6ft (120 x 180cm) walls are made up of slabs, and so when marbling a wall imitate the joins rather than painting in long unbroken runs.

Before you begin, study the patterning and colouration of real marble. Make some sketches so that when you come to execute the pattern in paint you can make your movements quick and sure.

It is a good idea at first to keep the colours of the base coat, glaze and veining fairly close in hue and intensity in order to give some coherence to the final effect. Too much contrast between elements in the pattern can be overpowering.

Although the traditional method (and the one giving the most realistic results) involves laying an oil glaze over a base coat (also of oil paint) and figuring the veins in artists' oils or oil crayon, water-based paints can also be used.

SEQUENCE FOR WATER GLAZE

An alternative, perhaps easier method, is to work with water-based glazes over a base coat of vinyl silk or eggshell paint. The basic sequence is:

1. Brush the base coat using criss-cross strokes in order to get the smoothest finish possible. Put on two or three coats, lightly sanding between each coat when it is dry.
2. Make up a glaze of four parts water to one part emulsion under-coat tinted with artists' gouache or acrylic.
3. Sponge on glaze and allow to dry. Add further coats of glaze (allowing each to dry before adding another) until you reach the soft cloudy background colouring of marble.
4. In a saucer or on a palette mix artists' acrylic and a little water and take some up with the tip of a goose feather or a sable brush.
5. Draw in the thickest of the veining, using a shaky irregular stroke.
6. When the veining is dry sponge on another coat of glaze to soften the veining.
7. When the glaze is dry use a finer

brush or feather to draw in the finer veins in a complementary tone of acrylic.
8. Glaze in a complementary tone to the previous glazes, veining and base coat.
9. Draw in the most delicate veins, using a very fine artists' brush. Seal the surface with a coat of gloss polyurethane.

SEQUENCE FOR OIL GLAZE

1. When the base coat is dry, apply random drifts of tinted oil glaze, leaving space for the second and third colours. These subsequent colours must be applied while the first colour is still wet, to enable the colours to blend.
2. With a stippling motion, brush and blend the colours until there is no distinct line where they meet.
3. To further soften the effect use a dry, lint-free cloth and gently dab the surface, breaking up the colours.
4. Soften the whole surface with a softening brush, preferably of badger hair.
5. Draw a feather dipped in white spirit through the glaze to open up areas in the background and give added depth.
6. Using another feather, apply dark complementary colours from a palette of neat artists' oils. Draw in the veining in darker colours. Study the veining in real marble before tackling this stage.
7. After further ragging and softening (see steps 3 and 4), use an oil-based crayon to draw in veins that dip below the surface in places.
8. Allow the finished marbling to dry for at least 24 hours and then protect it with one or two coats of clear, satin-finish polyurethane varnish.

MARBLING USING AN OIL GLAZE

1. *Working on a dried eggshell base, apply random drifts of tinted oil glaze, leaving space for the second and third colours. The subsequent colours must be applied while the first colour is still wet, to enable the colours to blend.*

2. *With a stippling motion, blend the colours until there is no distinct line where they meet.*

5. *Draw a feather dipped in white spirit through the glaze to open up areas in the background and give an added depth.*

6. *Now, using a feather, apply darker complementary colours from a palette of neat artists' oil paint. Draw in veins of the darker colours. It is advisable to look at examples of real marble before applying the veins.*

3. *To further soften the effect use a dry, lint-free cloth and softly dab the surface, breaking up the colours.*

4. *At this stage soften the whole surface with a softening brush, using a badger-hair brush if you have one.*

7. *After further ragging and softening (see previous stages), use an oil-based crayon to accentuate the fact that some veins are not just on the surface, but dip below it in places.*

8. *Allow the finished marbling to dry for at least 24 hours and then protect it by applying one or two coats of clear, satin-coat polyurethane varnish.*

WALLCOVERING

Of all the decorative wall treatments, no other can transform a room as quickly as wallcovering (a term that has superseded 'wallpapering' as increasingly wallcoverings have more to do with vinyl and other plastics than with paper).

Almost all of us, at one time or another will hang wallcovering, but not without a little trepidation. What about those bubbles, the misaligned strips, those awkward corners, or the daunting prospect of the ceiling and the stairwell? These are areas in which good preparation and careful planning will cut the problems down to size.

Wallcovering is not something to be rushed. Patience and organization are essential. The beginner, unnerved by the thought of tackling a large room, will often mistakenly imagine that a small room such as a bathroom is the best place to start. It is the worst. Too many corners, the confined space, and all those fiddly fixtures to be papered around make it one of the most difficult. Better to choose as large and regularly shaped a room as possible. Not only will it be technically easier to handle but it can also be covered comparatively quickly – a tremendous psychological boost to the novice. Choose a small, non-directional pattern rather than one with a complicated horizontal or drop pattern that will need more careful matching. Use good-quality paper that will resist wrinkling and tearing

CHOOSING THE WALLCOVERING

Although your first consideration may be purely aesthetic – does the colour and pattern look good? – there are other important functional considerations to bear in mind. If the surface to be covered is likely to need a fair bit of cleaning, say from children's grubby fingers or in a kitchen, then a scrubbable vinyl covering (or at least a washable vinyl-coated paper) will be preferable to a simple untreated wallpaper.

If the surface is less than perfect you may want to help disguise it with a small busy pattern or perhaps a relief (embossed) wallcovering that will distract the eye. Do not use regular vertical stripes or reflecting surfaces such as metallic foil, as these tend to accentuate unevenness.

COLOUR VARIATIONS

Wallcoverings are either machine printed or, in the case of more expensive papers, hand blocked. Coverings that are machine printed will have uniform colour from roll to roll as long as those rolls come from the same printing batch. Manufacturers put a batch number on each roll, and you should check your rolls to ensure they were printed together. Rolls from other printing batches may have slight colour variations. Hand-printed papers cannot have the same colour uniformity as machine printed, so that there may be slight colour variations from roll to roll. This is not necessarily a disaster as hand-printed papers are meant to have the charm of slight unevenness of colouring.

GUIDELINES BEFORE BUYING

* Take samples of wallcovering home to see the colour and pattern in the conditions in which it will be hung. If you cannot get a loose sample you may have to pay a small refundable deposit to take home a book of samples.
* Check whether the shop will refund you for unused rolls (although it is always better to buy an extra roll).
* Do the rolls, if machine printed, come from the same printing batch?
* Are the rolls in good condition? Check that the roll ends have not been damaged by careless handling or storage.

TYPES OF WALLCOVERING

Printed papers Machine-printed papers are the cheapest and most widely available type, offering the widest choice of patterns and colours. Although often spongeable, they are less suited to areas of heavy use such as kitchens and children's rooms. Hand-printed papers are more expensive and may have irregularities of colour and size.

Relief papers These have embossed surfaces, and are good for camouflaging imperfect surfaces. There are various types, sold under the names of, for example, Anaglypta (embossed paper); Super-glypta (cotton fibre); Vinaglypta (embossed vinyl). When hanging these wallcoverings, line the wall and apply a heavy-duty paste generously to the paper backing. Allow the paste to soak into the backing. Do not roller the joins as this will flatten the embossing; dab them with a stiff brush.

Paper-backed vinyl Vinyl film is heat-fused to a paper backing to give a surface highly resistant to stains and scrubbing. Paste as you would for conventional wallpaper, using a fungicide paste. Butt-join strips and smooth them with a damp sponge. Where edges overlap (on corners for example) use double-cut seams (see page 91).

Foamed vinyl Also known as 'blown' or 'sculptured' vinyl (trade name 'Novamura'). It is often styled to look like ceramic tiles or brick. Paste the wall with the manufacturer's recommended adhesive and work straight from the roll. Make sure there is plenty of adhesive along the edges as this type of covering has a tendency to curl.

Washables Printed paper coated with a thin plastic film. Use a fungicide paste and hang in the ordinary way. If the edges curl use a seam roller (as long as the wallcovering is not embossed).

Metallic Foils Will advertise any imperfections on the underlying surface and some may conduct electricity so should not be used near electrical outlets. Use a fungicide paste either on the wall itself or on the paper backing the foil.

Woodchip Slivers of wood are sandwiched between a paper backing and a thin surface paper. A good camouflaging covering that is fairly easy to hang. Trimming can be difficult (use a very sharp Stanley knife).

Flock A raised pile of wool, silk or synthetic fibre on a paper backing. When hanging it, protect the pile with lining paper and smooth out with a paperhanger's brush. Use double-cut seams (see page 91) to make joins.

Paper-backed fabrics These include hessian, felt, silk, or wool fused to a paper backing. They may need special adhesives (usually applied to the wall) which will be recommended by the manufacturer. Care should be taken to keep adhesives or paste off the fabric surface (cover the pasting table with lining paper to protect the delicate surface of the covering). If edges are not machine-trimmed, use the double-cut seam technique (page 91) and smooth down carefully with a paperhanger's brush.

If the rolls are heavy slide a pole through the centre and rest the ends on two stepladders. Start at the bottom of the wall and smooth upwards.

Expanded polystyrene Apply the special adhesive to the wall and allow it to set according to the manufacturer's instructions. Hang the covering straight from the roll, smoothing it lightly with your hand. Lightly roller with a dry, clean paint roller.

Fabrics see pages 102-103.
Ready-pasted see page 91.

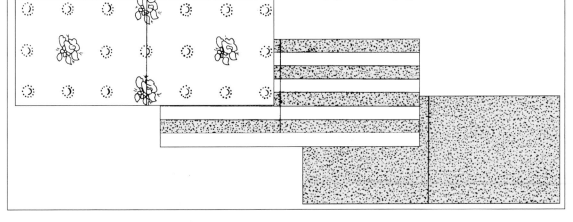

Above: *Borders and friezes offer good ways to create visual focal points as well as altering the perceived height of rooms. See also page 100.*

Right: *This room has a number of awkward angles that can cause problems when fixing wallcovering. See pages 92–97 for solutions. For tackling ceilings see pages 100–101.*

EQUIPMENT

The tools needed for wallcovering are neither extensive nor too expensive. Some can even be improvised quite easily. For example, a dining table will double as a pasting table providing it is about 6ft (2m) long and at least 21in (53cm) wide. If you do not want to pay for a top-of-the-range retractable bob, make your own plumb bob with a small weight tied to the end of a length of string. A wide paint brush will substitute for a paste brush.

Although ordinary household scissors can be used in place of long-bladed paperhanger's shears, the purpose-made shears will not only give a longer and cleaner cut, but will also speed up the job. Whichever you use, make sure they are sharp. Blunt scissors will tend to tear the wallcovering. Similarly with a Stanley or trimming knife, stock up on plenty of new blades, and change them often.

An ordinary plastic bucket with a piece of string tied across it makes an excellent paste bucket, complete with rest for the paste brush.

Clean paste drips and splashes from woodwork and other surfaces before they dry and become difficult to remove; paste that is left to dry on wallcovering will discolour it, so have clean rags and a sponge, together with another bucket of clean water, to hand. When you have finished, clean up equipment with fresh warm water.

See also steam stripper (page 85).

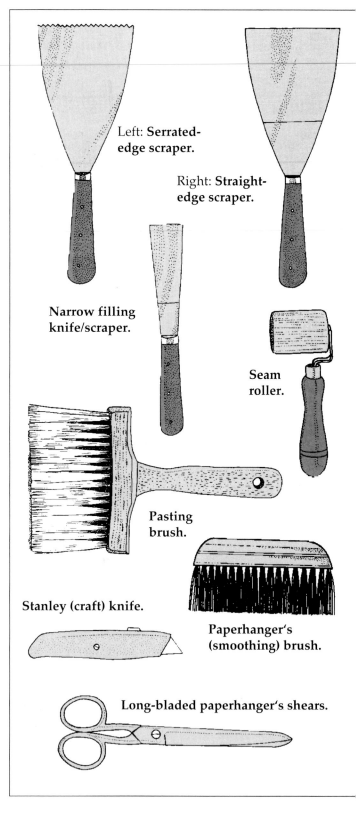

Left: **Serrated-edge scraper.**

Right: **Straight-edge scraper.**

Narrow filling knife/scraper.

Seam roller.

Pasting brush.

Stanley (craft) knife.

Paperhanger's (smoothing) brush.

Long-bladed paperhanger's shears.

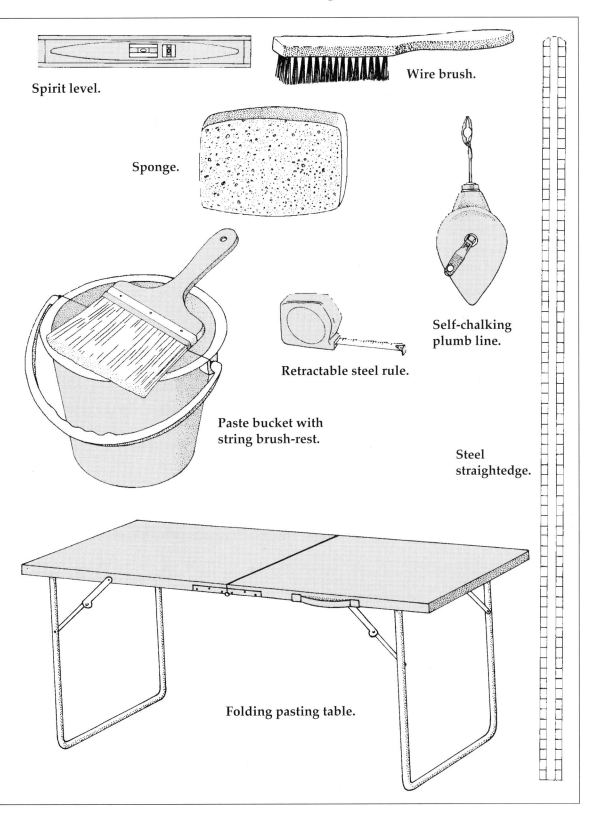

Spirit level.

Wire brush.

Sponge.

Self-chalking
plumb line.

Retractable steel rule.

Paste bucket with
string brush-rest.

Steel
straightedge.

Folding pasting table.

PREPARATION

If you intend to redecorate a room completely, then all woodwork and ceiling painting or papering should be completed first. Clear the room of as much furniture as possible and move what remains into the centre. Get rid of as much clutter as you can. Good organisation will not only make the job go more smoothly but will also prevent accidents such as stumbling over objects while carrying lengths of wallcovering. Do not leave wallcovering trimmings on the floor – they can be as treacherous as banana skins if trodden on.

ESTIMATING

Nothing is more frustrating than running out of wallcovering before a job is completed, only to find that the stockist has no more from the same printing batch or the manufacturer has discontinued the line.

Most coverings are sold in rolls 11yds (10.5m) long and 21in (53cm) wide. A roll will cover an area approximately 6½ sq yds (5.3 sq m). There will always be some waste, particularly so with large drop patterns where you can lose more paper than usual in matching the pattern. Order an extra roll to compensate. An extra roll may also come in handy for future repairs. Use the chart to work out how many rolls you will need according to the total perimeter measurement and wall height.

When estimating for ceilings, take the area of the floor and add any extra areas such as soffits or dormer windows. Divide the area (in square metres) by five. This will give you the number of rolls needed with a little extra built in as a safety margin.

HOW MANY ROLLS?

		TOTAL MEASUREMENT OF ROOM PERIMETER, INCLUDING DOORS AND WINDOWS												
		9	10	11	12	13	14	15	16	17	18	19	20	metres
WALL HEIGHT FROM SKIRTINGBOARD		30	33	36	39	42	46	49	52	56	59	62	65	feet
metres	feet													
2.0 – 2.2	6½ –7¼	4	4	5	5	5	6	6	6	6	7	7	8	
2.2 – 2.4	7¼–7¾	4	4	5	5	6	6	6	7	7	8	8	9	
2.4 – 2.6	7¾ –8½	4	5	5	6	6	7	7	8	8	9	9	10	
2.6 – 2.8	8½ –9¼	5	5	6	6	7	7	8	8	9	9	10	11	
2.8 – 3.0	9¼–9¾	5	5	6	7	7	8	8	9	9	10	11	12	
3.0 – 3.2	9¾ –10½	6	7	7	8	9	9	10	11	11	12	12	13	
3.2 – 3.4	10½ –11	6	7	8	8	9	10	10	11	12	12	13	14	
3.4 – 3.6	11 –11¾	7	7	8	9	10	11	11	12	12	13	14	14	
3.6 – 3.8	11¾ –12½	7	8	9	9	10	11	12	12	13	14	14	15	

PASTE

Check the manufacturer's directions on the wallcovering label for the most suitable paste. Ordinary papers need a cold-water cellulose paste made up from a powder. The heavier the paper, the thicker should be the paste. Always follow the mixing instructions on the packet.

Vinyls and other plastic-coated papers not only need a stronger paste but one that contains a fungicide. Vinyl- and plastic-coated papers trap the paste's moisture and prevent it from drying out very quickly. Unless prevented by a fungicide, mould can grow under the covering. Ordinary paste will not effectively stick overlapping seams of vinyl, and a special adhesive will have to be used.

PREVIOUSLY PAINTED WALLS

If the surface is in good condition and has been painted with an emulsion, it should be washed down with a water and detergent or sugar soap solution to remove any grease. Whitewash or distemper should be removed completely by scrubbing with water. If left it could flake and cause the wallcovering to lift off. When the surface is dry, seal the plaster with a thinned coat of plaster-binder-sealer.

Gloss and sheen finishes will not provide a sufficient grip for the paste and should be rubbed down with coarse sandpaper to provide a key.

NEW PLASTER

When the plaster is completely dry, fill any holes and cracks with a filling compound. Seal the plaster with a thinned coat of plaster-binder-sealer, otherwise the unsealed plaster will absorb the paste, causing the wall-covering to lift and bubble. Alternatively, brush on a liberal coat of size (paste diluted with about twice as much water). Apart from reducing porosity it also helps make it easier to manoeuvre the pasted wallcovering when you are fitting it to the wall. If you are using a washable covering, remember to use a size containing fungicide.

BARE WOOD

Moisture in wallcovering paste will tend to lift the grain in bare wood, which will show through wallpaper. Prime the wood thoroughly with a liberal coat of oil-based wood primer. When this primer has dried, lightly rub it down with fine sandpaper. On large areas of bare wood hang lining paper horizontally.

STRIPPING OLD WALLCOVERING

Although it is possible to paper over existing wallcovering if it provides a sound base, it is preferable to strip it off. And certainly you should not try to add a new covering on top of more than one old one.

If you are to work over existing paper, tear away any detached strips and lightly sand the edges of the tear to feather them smooth. Sand down overlapping seams with medium sandpaper and stick back any curling corners with paste.

Ordinary wallpaper, as well as embossed and woodchip, are often the hardest to remove because they are solidly bonded to the surface. Paper-backed vinyl is easy because the vinyl surface can usually be peeled away by taking a top corner and pulling it down diagonally. Once the surface vinyl has been stripped you should be left with a sound paper base on which to hang wallcovering.

Foamed polyethylene or 'strippable' wallcovering is, as its name implies, the easiest of all to remove. It will peel away to leave a bare surface.

Dry stripping

Using a stripping knife or specialised stripping tool on old wallcovering is the most laborious of all the stripping methods. It is only really worthwhile if the old wallcovering is already lifting from the wall.

Slit the wallcovering and insert the blade of the stripping knife, lifting and sliding to remove the covering. You will probably have to use a narrow-bladed knife on more obstinate wallcovering and, unless you are very lucky, there will always be tags and strips of paper left on the wall. These will have to be rubbed down with sandpaper.

One of the circumstances in which you may have to use dry stripping is when removing wallcovering from plasterboard. Soaking, chemical and steam-stripping techniques (see below) can damage the paper coating of the plasterboard and the plaster core. Unless you are sure that the plasterboard has been sealed with a primer (and is therefore protected against moisture) dry stripping may be the only option. In this case, you may well want to make every effort to use the existing covering as a base for the new.

Soaking

Porous wallpaper (that is, not one covered with vinyl or plastic coating) can be soaked with a solution of washing-up liquid and water (warm water will help speed up the process).

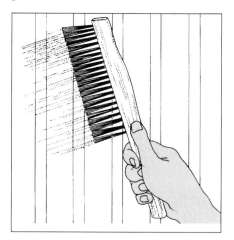

First score the paper all over with a serrated scraper or a wire brush. This will allow the soaking solution to penetrate the paper. Sponge or brush on the solution liberally, and start to strip after the paper has had time to thoroughly soak up the solution and is wet (10-20 minutes). You may need to re-soak the old paper but time spent on several soakings will be rewarded when you come to strip.

If you have to work close to electrical fittings make sure the power has been turned off and is not turned on again until the stripping has been finished and the surface is dry.

Chemical stripping

Chemical wallpaper removers usually come in powder form and have to be dissolved in water according to the manufacturer's instructions (one packet will comfortably deal with a 13ft (4m) x 16ft (5m) room). They contain quite caustic chemicals, so wear rubber gloves. As with soaking, score the wallcovering and brush on the solution, allowing about 30 minutes for the chemicals to start loosening the paste.

Apply another coat of stripper and lift off the old wallcovering with a broad-bladed stripping knife. If the wallcovering is still resistant, soak again (being careful to protect flooring that can be discoloured by chemical stripper). If you are not making much headway you will have to use the most efficient method of all – steam stripping.

Steam stripping

Steam stripping is the fastest way to remove all types of old wallcovering. If you have a lot of stripping to do it may be more economical to buy a machine from a DIY outlet or wallcovering supplier. For less extensive jobs, hiring will probably be the answer. Some multi-purpose carpet steam cleaners are also adaptable for use as steam strippers.

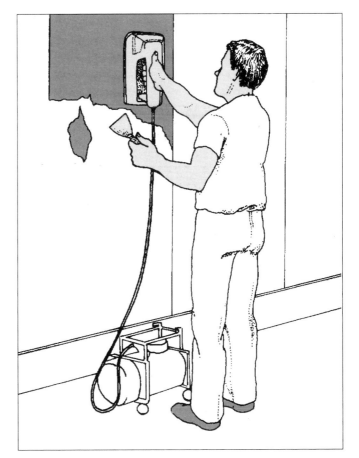

Using a steam stripper.

Most purpose-built strippers have a water tank that is filled with cold or hot water (always make sure the machine is unplugged from an electrical socket before filling). The water tank is connected by a rubber tube to a hand-held plate. As the water is boiled in the tank, steam will emerge from the holes in the face of the plate. The plate is then held firmly against the old wallcovering, without moving it, for about 30 seconds to two minutes, depending on the porosity of the wallcovering. Do not hold the plate in one place for too long, particularly if the plaster is suspect. Such plaster can 'blow' (balloon out and break up) if subjected to too much steam. Ordinary, untreated papers will take less time than washable coverings.

LINING PAPER

If the surface you intend to paper is rough (or if you are going to use a high-quality wallcovering), it may be advisable to provide a solid base for the final wallcovering by hanging strips of lining paper (an inexpensive white paper). Lining paper is always hung horizontally so that its seams will not interfere with the seams of the final wallcovering.

Mark a horizontal guideline one width's distance from the ceiling. Start hanging the lining paper at the top of the wall and work down, allowing a 2in (50mm) overlap around corners. Use the same paste as for the final wallcovering.

Hang lining paper horizontally so that its seams cannot clash with the seams of the final wallcovering.

On badly damaged walls you may want to hang two layers of lining paper; one vertically, one horizontally. The problem here, though, is that you now have two underlying layers to which the final wallcovering must adhere. It might be better to undertake the repairs to the wall that the lining paper is to hide.

WHERE TO START

You would be very lucky indeed for the perimeter measurement of the room to be papered to be exactly divisible by the width of the roll of wallcovering, thus avoiding any mismatch. With almost all rooms there will be points of mismatch, and you should plan ahead to make them as inconspicuous as possible.

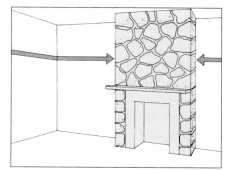

If the wall surface is broken by a feature such as a fireplace, end the job on either side.

If the room has an obvious focal point, such as a fireplace, it should determine the starting point, for this is where the eye is first drawn when entering the room. It is particularly important if you are using a pattern that needs to be matched that the matching is perfect at the focal point.

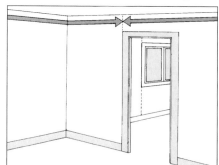

Plan to end the job at a point where the mismatch will be least obvious.

By measuring rolls radiating out from the centre line of the focal point you will be able to plan to end the job at the least conspicuous part of the room – by a door or window, for example, or perhaps in a tucked-away corner.

If there is a feature in the room which breaks up the surface - a built-in cupboard or brick chimney breast, for example – then start hanging at the opposite end of the room and work towards the feature. If the room has no dominant focal point, start the wallcovering in the middle of the longest wall.

AVOIDING UNSIGHTLY STRIPS

Whether you are working towards a corner, around windows, doors or fireplaces, plan the starting roll so that you do not end up with strips at the corners of less than 6in (150mm). Either centre the starting roll on the centre line or start with the roll edge on the centre line – whichever eliminates a strip of less than 6in (50mm) at the wall's corner.

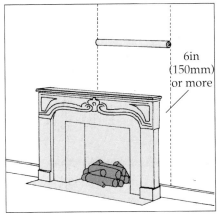

Have the left edge of the roll on the centre line as long as the strip on the right of the fireplace is more than 6in (150mm).

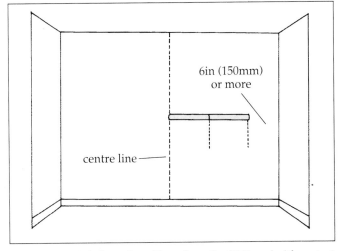

To avoid unsightly strips of less than 6in (150mm) either start the edge of the first roll at the centre line (above) or start with the roll centred on the line (below).

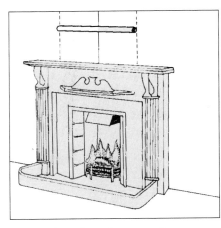

Centre the roll on the centre line to eliminate strips at side of less than 6in (150mm).

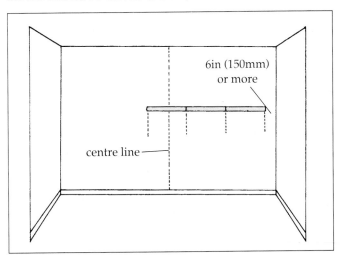

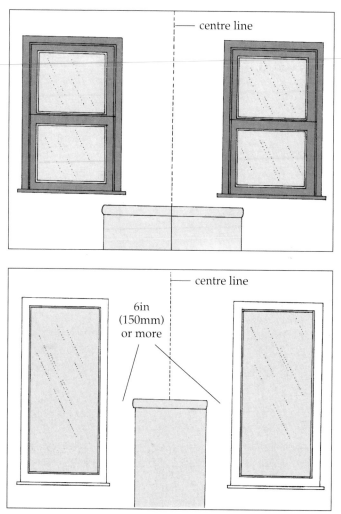

centre line

centre line

6in
(150mm)
or more

*Centre the seam between the windows (top), or centre the roll
between the windows (above).*

Right: *Here the
roll is centred at
the mid-point of
the window
which results in a
strip down the
side of more than
6in (150mm).*

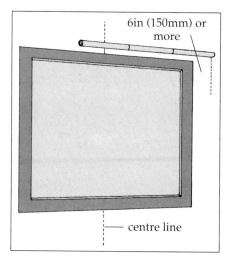

6in (150mm) or
more

centre line

GETTING IT STRAIGHT

It is critically important to the
outcome of the whole job that the first
length of wallcovering be hung truly
vertical. All houses have some degree
of misalignment between surfaces,
and if you hang wallcovering to align
with, for example, the ceiling, the
misalignment will become more and
more obvious as you proceed around
the walls.

A carpenter's spirit level will
indicate true horizontals and verticals,
but if you do not have a spirit level it
is easy to make your own plumb bob.
Attach a small weight to a length of
string which has a loop tied at the free
end. Hang the string by the loop from
a tack near the top of the wall. When
the weight comes to a standstill make
a series of faint pencil marks behind
the string (being careful not to move

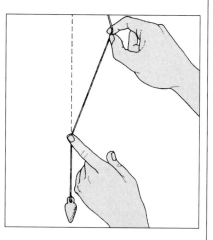

it) and join them up to make a vertical
guideline. Alternatively, rub chalk
along the string before you hang it on
the tack. When the bob has come to
rest, pull it down slightly until the
string is taut. With your free hand
pull the string back like a bowstring
and release it so that it snaps against
the wall and leaves a chalk line. More
sophisticated plumb bobs have a
retractable string and chalk-dust
reservoir.

BEFORE PASTING

Before measuring out your lengths of wallcovering, ascertain which way up the pattern should go. It sounds obvious, but it is an easy mistake to make. Having measured the height of the wall to be covered, add 2in (50mm) top and bottom for trimming at the ceiling and skirting-board. If you are working with horizontal or dropped patterns that need matching, measure, match and cut a series of lengths. Stack the lengths flat and in sequence so that you can keep up the momentum once you start pasting and hanging.

It will also help to speed things up if you mark off the pasting table with guidelines at 1ft (30cm) and 6in (150mm) intervals.

PASTING

Ensure that the surface of the pasting table is scrupulously clean and free of anything such as splinters or nail heads that could snag and tear the covering. Place your wallcovering pattern-side down and, using a broad pasting brush (a broad paint brush or roller will do) lay on an even, generous coat of paste, starting at the centre and working towards the edges. Make sure the whole surface is covered, particularly the edges. The length will now have to be folded ('booked').

BOOKING

Once the wallcovering has been pasted, allow about five minutes for it to absorb the paste. Fold the two outer ends over until they meet in the centre, taking care not to crease the folds. The length can then be carried draped over one arm.

For very long lengths (such as those needed for ceilings or the long drops of stairwells) fold the paper concertina fashion, paste against paste.

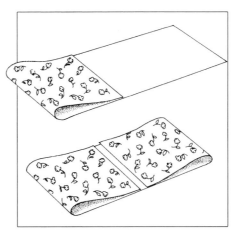

A simple way to book pasted lengths.

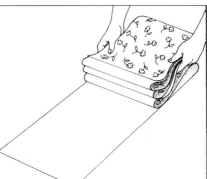

A concertina fold for longer lengths such as those for stairwells and ceilings.

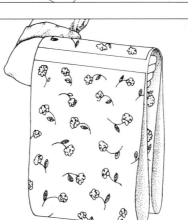

Carrying pasted and booked wallcovering

THE FIRST STRIP

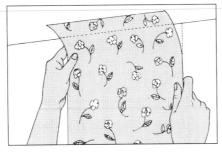

1. Offer the top edge of the paper up to the top of the wall (overlapping by 2in/50mm) and allow the booked length to gently unfold. Smooth out the top of the length to hold it in place. Manoeuvre the paper until one edge lines up with the plumb line.

2. Brush the paper from the centre to the edges to expel any trapped air pockets.

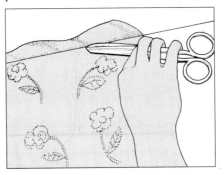

3. Run the back of the scissors along the paper where it meets the ceiling to give a clean crease.

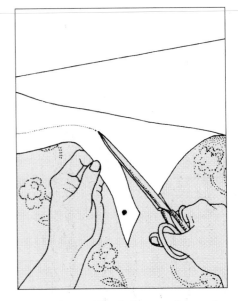

4. Gently peel back the overlap at the ceiling and cut along the crease with sharp, long-bladed scissors.
5. Brush back the edges flush to the ceiling.
6. Repeat the creasing and cutting sequence at the skirtingboard overlap.
7. Wash off any paste on skirtingboards or ceilings.

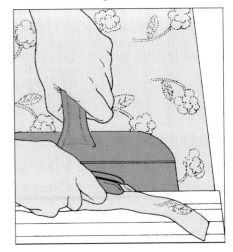

Another trimming technique using a broad knife and a sharp Stanley knife.

THE SECOND STRIP

1. Offer up the second strip and secure it as described in step one of the First Strip (page 90).

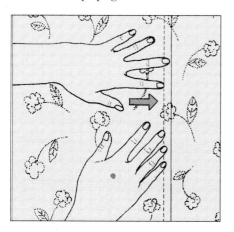

2. Using widely spread fingers to spread the pressure and prevent tearing, slide the edge of the paper until it butts up against the first strip. Check the whole drop to make sure there is neat butting.

3. Working from the centre to the edges, smooth out any excess air.

4. Roll over the seam between the two strips with a seam roller (or even with your finger wrapped in a clean cloth). Do not put too much pressure on the seam roller or it may leave 'tram lines'. Seam rollers should not be used on relief wallcoverings as they will flatten the relief pattern.

DOUBLE-CUT SEAMS

Although butt seams are the easiest, there may be occasions when you will need to double-cut a seam in order to make a clean join (for example, when papering around an outside corner which is out of vertical). Although a mismatch is almost inevitable, a double-cut seam will look neater than a thick wodge of overlapped paper.

Overlap one strip with another by about ½in (12mm). Using a straightedge and a sharp Stanley knife (dull blades will tear the paper) cut down through the centre of the overlap, cutting through both layers of wallcovering. Peel off the strip from the outer piece of the overlap. Lift back the overlap and peel away the strip from the underlying piece of wallcovering. Smooth back the edges and run over them with a seam roller to make a close-fitting butt join.

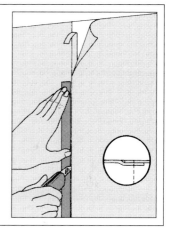

PREPASTED WALLCOVERING

Prepasted wallcovering comes with a backing of dried paste. The whole roll needs to be soaked in water in order to activate the paste. Often prepasted wallcovering comes with its own water trough, although any container suitably long and deep enough to completely cover the roll will do. Place the trough on the floor at one end of the pasting table. Fill it sufficiently full of water to cover the roll of wallcovering. Soak the wallcovering for about 15 seconds (or follow the manufacturer's instructions). Taking the corners of the leading edge in both hands, gently unroll the covering and lay it, pattern side down, on the pasting table. Alternatively, some manufacturers recommend hanging the wallcovering straight from the trough on to the wall.

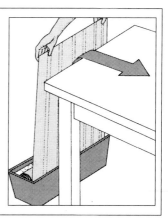

AWKWARD SPACES

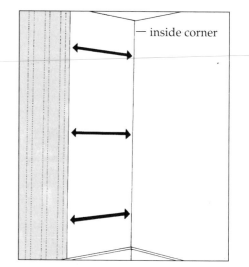

— inside corner

INSIDE CORNERS

1. As walls may not be plumb, you will need to make three width measurements (top, middle, bottom) from the last strip to the inside corner. Add 1in (25mm) to the widest measurement. This gives an overlap that will go round the corner on to the adjacent wall.

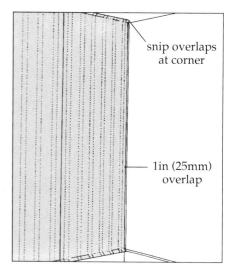

snip overlaps at corner

1in (25mm) overlap

2. Cut the strip to the width required (pasting and booking in the normal way) and butt up the machine-cut edge of the new strip to the previous strip, smoothing out the new strip towards the corner. To prevent creasing at the corner, cut little triangular wedges out of the top and bottom overlap where they meet the corner. The 1in (25mm) overlap should now lie flat on the adjacent wall.

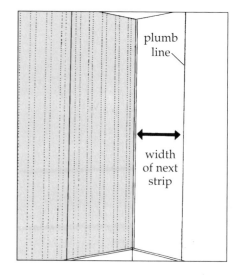

plumb line

width of next strip

3. Mark a plumb line on the adjacent wall the width of a roll plus ½ in (12mm). This will ensure that the first strip you hang on the adjacent wall will cover most of the overlap.

OUTSIDE CORNERS

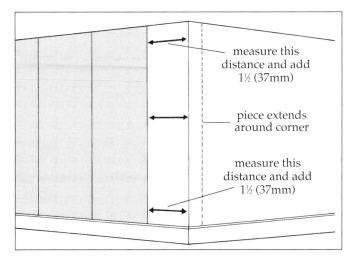

measure this distance and add 1½ (37mm)

piece extends around corner

measure this distance and add 1½ (37mm)

1. Make three measurements (top, middle, bottom) from the edge of the last strip to the corner. Add 1½in (27mm) to the widest measurement to provide an overlap to go round the corner.

2. Measure and cut a strip of wallcovering, paste and book it in the usual way. Hang it with the machine-cut edge butted up to the previous strip.

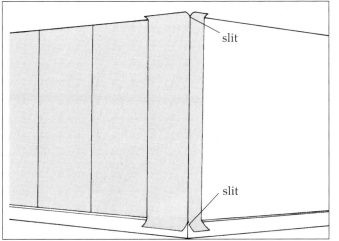

slit

slit

3. Smooth the strip out towards the corner. When the covering reaches the corner cut little triangular wedges at the top and foot of the wallcovering so that it will go round the corner without creasing.

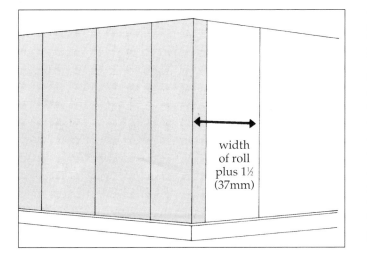

width of roll plus 1½ (37mm)

4. Mark a vertical plumb line on the adjacent wall the width of a roll plus ½ in (12mm) away from the corner. This will ensure the first strip on the adjacent wall covers most of the overlap from the previous wall. If the overlapped join is too thick and unsightly, use a double-cut seam (see page 91). If you are using a vinyl wallcovering you will have to use a double-cut seam because vinyl will not adhere to vinyl. Relief papers will also need a double-cut seam because they are usually too bulky to make a neat overlap join.

DOORWAYS

Allow about 3in (75mm) of excess wallcovering to hang over the door frame. Make diagonal cuts towards the outside corner of the door frame and run the back of a pair of scissors down the wallcovering at the point where wall and door frame meet. Lift the wallcovering away from the frame and cut down the crease with sharp, long-bladed scissors. Alternatively use a straightedge and Stanley knife to trim the wallcovering at the frame.

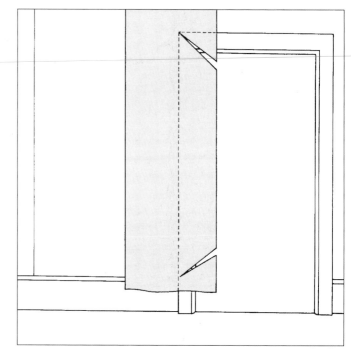

LIGHT SWITCHES

1. Paper over the switch and mark the centre of the switch on the wallcovering. Cut slits from the centre to each of the corners. This will leave four flaps of wallcovering hanging over the switch.

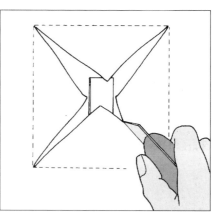

2. Turn off the electricity. Cut off the flaps with a Stanley knife or scissors and trim the wallcovering flush with the switch. Alternatively, loosen the switch cover and tuck a little overlap wallcovering behind the switch cover. Screw back the switch cover to make a neat join.

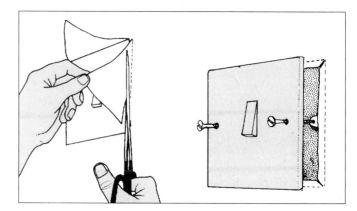

RECESSED WINDOWS

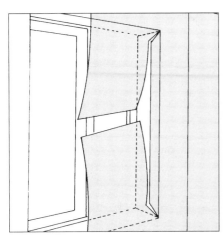

1. Allow excess paper to hang over part of the window space. Cut a horizontal line to within 1in (25mm) of the wall edge. Cut up vertically and then across diagonally to the outside corner of the recess. Repeat the vertical and diagonal cuts to the bottom corner.

2. Paste the overlap flaps to the inside of the recess. Cut strips to paste on the inside of the recess to within ¼in (6mm) of the outside edges.

PAPERING AROUND A HANDBASIN

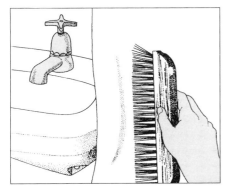

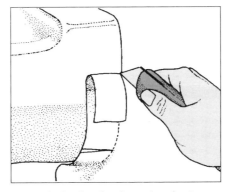

1. Brush the wallcovering to the edge of the basin allowing about 2in (50mm) to overlap the basin side. Cut three horizontal slits. The top one should be about ½in (12mm) above the top of the basin, the bottom about ½in (12mm) above the basin base, the centre to within about ½in (12mm) of the wall. The wallcovering can now be smoothed in to follow the contour of the basin.

2. With the back of a pair of scissors crease the excess wallcovering around the contour of the basin and either trim along the crease with a sharp Stanley knife or peel back the wallcovering and trim along the crease with a pair of scissors. Brush the wallcovering back flush to the basin.

ARCHES

1. Allow about 2in (50mm) of wallcovering to overhang the arch.

2. Cut triangular snips from the overhung paper, spacing them closer together where the curve is tightest. Paste the flaps to the inside of the arch.

3. Paste a strip of wallcovering (cut about ½ in/12mm narrower than the inside of the arch) to the inside of the arch to cover the flaps.

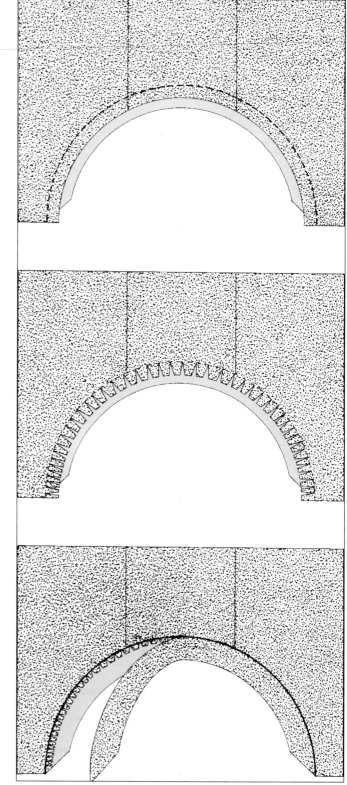

RADIATORS

Some modern radiators can be lowered for easy access to the wall. Most, however, cannot be moved easily.

1. Measure and cut long narrow strips from the wallcovering to allow it to drop on either side of the radiator's support brackets (usually about (1¼in/30mm wide). Push the wallcovering down behind the radiator using a flat wooden batten.

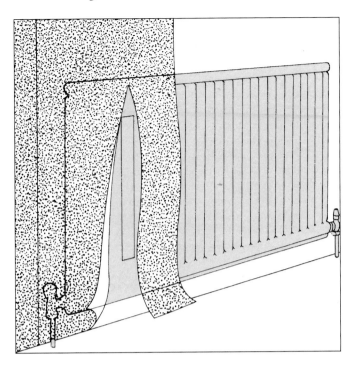

2. With the batten, crease the bottom of the wallcovering where it meets the skirtingboard. Pull the wallcovering back up and trim off along the crease. Replace the wallcovering, smoothing it with the batten. You can also buy special radiator rollers (used for painting behind radiators) that will help smooth the wallcovering.

Above: *A combination of painted marble effect (see pages 72-75)
and wallcovering that incorporates a decorative frieze (see page 100).
Use a fungicide paste when hanging wallcovering in rooms such as
bathrooms and kitchens that can be steamy. Moisture behind
wallcovering can lead to fungal growth.*

Right: *Before tackling a stairwell it is important to erect a stable and
safe working platform (see page 17). See page 104 for the techniques
of hanging wallcovering in stairwells.*

BORDERS AND FRIEZES

Decorative paper borders and friezes have increased in popularity over the last few years. They can give a striking accent to a room at ceiling or waist level, be used to frame fireplaces, windows or doorways, and also help improve the proportions of a room. For example, high ceilings can be 'lowered' by a frieze and featureless, boxy rooms can be given focal points by the creation of panels within borders.

Borders and friezes come in a wide range of widths from ¾in (18mm) up to 18in (450mm). Roll lengths may vary but a standard length is 29ft (9m). Some paper borders and friezes will need to be pasted in the normal way, although many now come ready-pasted and will only need to be soaked in water to activate the adhesive. If you intend to put a border or frieze over vinyl paper you will need to use special vinyl adhesive.

Whether you are hanging a frieze at ceiling level or a border at waist level, it is essential that it looks horizontal and runs parallel to, for example, the ceiling, picture rail or skirtingboard. As walls and ceilings may be out of alignment a spirit level will not be much help. Measure down from the ceiling or picture rail, or up from the skirtingboard (depending which is nearer where you want to run your frieze or border) at regular intervals to establish a base line. Join up these measurment marks with a faint pencil line.

When the strips have been measured and pasted, book them in concertina-type folds, being careful not to crease the folds. This will make it easier to feed out the strip in one hand while aligning and smoothing it with the other. There's no doubt, though, that this is a job much better handled by two people, one holding and feeding the booked strip, the other aligning and smoothing.

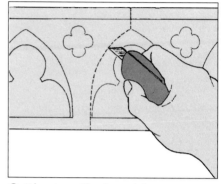

Cutting two stips to match.

When hanging across long stretches of wall, start with a corner overlap to minimise the mismatch. If a join mid-wall cannot be avoided, cut at as inconspicuous a part of the pattern as you can. If the pattern has a strong motif cut around the outline of the motif and fit the two strips together like a jigsaw puzzle, thus minimising the join.

Ensure that any stray paste is wiped up immediately. Run over the edges and joins with a seam roller for a clean finish.

CEILINGS

It is best to tackle ceilings before walls, and it is certainly one of those jobs made much easier with two people working on it.

It is important to have an adequate and safe platform from which to work. Nothing is more frustrating – and dangerous – than trying to cover a ceiling from one swaying stepladder. Make a proper platform from two stepladders and planks (see page 17).

If you are an inexperienced decorator it is certainly advisable to work with a small non-directional pattern that will avoid the fiddly matching and fitting of larger patterns.

Procedure

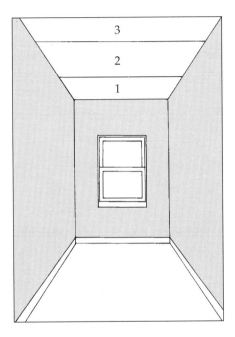

Measure and cut all the lengths you will need and stack them. Paste and book each length concertina-fashion as you need it.

With a helper holding the booked paper (supported with a spare roll of paper or cardboard roll) behind you, fit the paper to the guideline and, moving back slowly, brush out air pockets from the centre of the paper to the edges.

Plan to hang the paper parallel to, and starting at, the window wall (after the first piece is hung you will be able to work back into the room with the window, and the light, behind you). If the room has no window, hang the paper across the shortest dimension. The aim is to work with the shortest, and therefore least cumbersome, lengths of paper possible.

Mark a guideline the width of the roll away from the starting wall. Allow a 2in (50mm) overlap on the walls at either end. These overlaps will either be covered when you paper the walls or they will be trimmed.

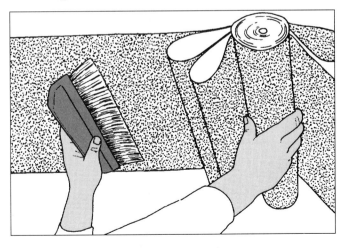

If you have to work alone, support the booked length with a cardboard roll or spare roll of paper.

HANGING FABRIC

Top: *Fabric fixed directly to the wall.*
Above: *Folds of fabric hanging from track.*

SHIRRING

Fabric can be slotted on to wires, rods or laths that span the area to be hung and are fixed by brackets below the ceiling and above the skirtingboard or floor. Fabric is fed onto these supports and gathered ('shirred') into pleats. This method is best suited to lightweight materials such as muslin. You will need three times as much material as for taut fabric covering or conventional wall-covering.

DIRECT TO WALL

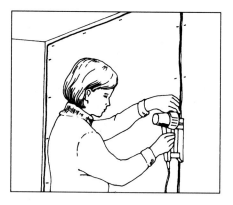

1. Using an industrial staple-gun (available from DIY shops), staple strips of polyester batting (available from upholstery fabric suppliers) directly to the wall (leaving a ¾in/19mm) gap all around the perimeter of the wall.
2. Cut lengths of fabric with a 2in (50mm) addition at top and bottom and sew enough lengths together (matching the pattern if necessary) to cover the wall (with about 2in /50mm extra for turning round inside corners).

TRACK SYSTEMS

The development of plastic mounting track has made the need for battening (creating a lattice of thin wooden laths to which fabric is stapled, practically obsolete. The track is pinned to the wall all around its perimeter and a tape on the track peeled away to expose an adhesive strip. The fabric is stuck on to the track and pressed into place. Once the final adjustments to the fabric's tension have been made, the edges of the fabric can be locked into place using the special tool usually provided with track systems.

3. Starting at a relatively inconspicuous place (alongside a door, for example) align as much of the top of the fabric to the ceiling line as you can manage and fix it with drawing pins.

4. Staple down the left-hand edge of the fabric (staple parallel to the door frame or wall from which you are starting at 2in/50mm intervals).

5. Remove the drawing pins and staple the top of the fabric as close to the ceiling or cornice as possible. Continue across the whole length of the wall, checking with a plumb line that the seams are falling truly vertical. Once you are sure the seam is hanging properly staple it at the bottom.

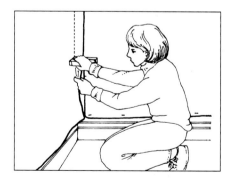

6. Smoothing the fabric out with your hand, staple along the bottom edge.

7. On outside corners, pull the fabric around as tightly as you can.

8. On inside corners, stretch the fabric as tightly into the corner as you can and staple the overlap to the adjacent wall as close in to the corner as you can manage. Take the next piece of fabric and lay it face down over the first (making sure the pattern matches as far as possible). You will now have edge to edge at the corner. With drawing pins, carefully align and fix the top of the second piece of fabric at the ceiling line and staple down through the edges of the two pieces of fabric. Run

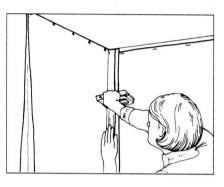

a length of upholsterer's tape down the join and staple it through both layers of fabric (illustration right). Remove the drawing pins and fold back the second piece of fabric, pulling it taut against the tape and pinning it along the ceiling line.

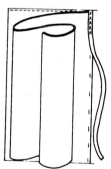

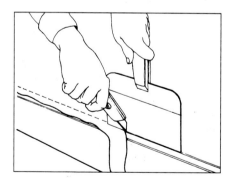

9. Trim off excess fabric at ceiling and floor or skirtingboard level with a broad knife and Stanley knife. Glue braid, or tack quarter-dowel along these edges for a neat finish.

Ceiling fixtures

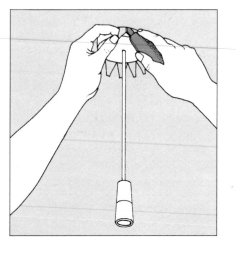

If a ceiling light falls in the middle of a strip, paper over it and mark its centre on the paper. Cut slits that will allow you to pass the light fitting through the paper. Make a series of cuts, radiating out from the centre until you find the paper sits snugly round the rose. Trim off the excess paper with a sharp Stanley knife.

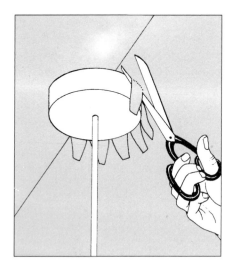

If the light fixture falls at the edge of a strip, cut a series of radial 'teeth' that will allow you to fit the paper to the outline of the rose. Trim off the excess paper with scissors or a Stanley knife.

STAIRWELLS

It is vitally important to work from an adequate and safe platform (see page 17). Handling long, pasted lengths of wallcovering is tiring, and very long lengths are also prone to swinging, stretching and tearing, so it will help greatly if you can work with someone to assist you.

For the beginner it is best to avoid horizontal and drop patterns that will need careful matching. Use small and non-directional patterns.

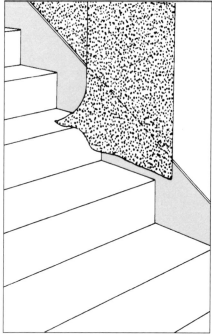

Start with the longest drop first and mark a guideline with a plumb bob (see page 96). Remember that where the covering meets the stair skirting-board you must cut the strip to its longest edge rather than its shortest. Measure, cut and stack all the strips you will need.

Use plenty of paste on long strips to prevent them drying out before you have had time to work down to the bottom.

RECTIFYING PROBLEMS

BLISTERS AND BUBBLES

Bubbles under the wallcovering can usually be avoided during the hanging process by ensuring that the wallcovering has been thoroughly pasted as well as carefully smoothed from the centre of the strip to its edges. Blisters and bubbles can also result from hanging on a surface that has not been properly sized or sealed, with the result that the paste is sucked into the surface. If however, you find air bubbles have been trapped when the wallcovering has dried (if you have small bubbles when the paper is still wet, they may disappear as the paper dries and stretches) cut small right-angled slits in the bubble to create a small flap. Try to hide the slits in the pattern, if possible. Repaste the flap and stick it

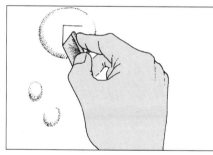

down, making sure all the air has been expelled.

WRINKLES AND CREASES

Wrinkles and creases are usually caused by a misalignment of the strip and cannot be cured by stretching and pulling the wallcovering. While the wallcovering is still wet, unpeel it from the wall and realign, smoothing it down carefully from top to bottom.

LIFTING SEAMS

Sometimes the edges of a strip have not been sufficiently pasted, or have dried out more quickly than the rest of the strip. Use a small brush to run paste under the seam. Press the seam down and brush it down firmly with a smoothing brush. Immediately wipe away any paste that may seep out.

PATCHING

This is a useful technique for disguising larger areas of damage.
1. Take a spare piece of wallcovering large enough to fit over the damaged area with a good overlap.
2. Match the pattern of the patch to the underlying wallcovering and fix the patch in place with masking tape.

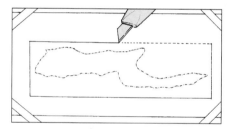

3. Using a sharp Stanley knife cut through both the patch and the underlying wallcovering. Remove the patch and strip away as much of the damaged area as you can.

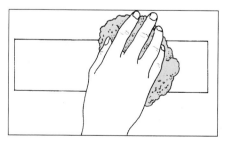

4. Paste the patch into the stripped area and smooth it firmly into place.

DECORATIVE MOULDINGS

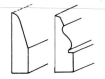

*Architrave –
plain, ogee*

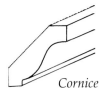

Cornice

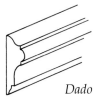

Dado

*Picture
rail*

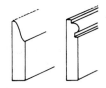

*Skirtingboard –
plain, moulded*

Original decorative moulding is still found in older houses (those built up to the First World War). Plasterwork is fairly fragile, yet seems to have survived the ordinary ravages of time, as well as the impulse to 'modernise' that particularly characterised the 1950s and '60s. Before about 1856 most plasterwork was solid and usually restricted to grander establishments. After that date the mixture of natural fibres and plaster opened the way to mass production. Today, decorative mouldings are available in their traditional materials of plaster and wood, but also in fibreglass and polystyrene. Cornices, dados and picture rails can help break up a large expanse of high wall (typically 9½ feet in a Victorian house) and can therefore help to 'lower' a high ceiling and pull colour schemes together.

Ceiling roses (the decorative moulding surrounding a ceiling light) are usually found in pre-1920 homes and, until the latter part of the last century, were made from solid plaster. Now, however, there is a wide range of fibrous plaster and expanded polystyrene reproductions available which can be fixed to the ceiling using adhesive recommended by the moulding manufacturer.

Cornices are the decorative plaster features at the junction of walls and ceilings. Many manufacturers now offer a wide range of styles of cornicing in fibrous plaster, or at the cheap end of the range, polystyrene or moulded plastic. Timber merchants often stock a range of softwood cornicing.

If you are fitting wood or fibrous plaster cornicing you may find it helpful to support each length with nails tacked into the wall below the cornice or, more elaborately, a thin piece of batten tacked to the wall on which the cornice can sit (wooden cornices have little 'give' along their length, so butting lengths together can be difficult because of walls out of true). The cornice itself should be seated in an adhesive recommended by the manufacturer and also nailed at 8in (200mm) intervals (countersink the nail heads below the surface of the cornice and fill the holes). Polystyrene cornice can be simply glued using the recommended adhesive, but as walls and ceilings are rarely at perfect right-angles they may need some support from nails, at least while the adhesive is drying.

Picture rails were originally always made of wood (and pictures suspended from them by cord or wire) but now that their role tends to be mainly purely decorative they are often made of fibrous plaster or even polystyrene. Traditionally they should be 1–1ft 8in (30–52cm) below the ceiling line and work particularly well in reducing the perceived height of lofty rooms. See cornices (above) for fixing details.

Dados or chair rails were originally functional – that is, they were used to protect walls and, more importantly, expensive wooden panelling or wainscotting, from being scuffed by chair backs. Dados are always wooden and are fixed (with countersunk nails or screws) 3–4ft (1–1.3m) from floor height. The space between the dado and the skirtingboard offers decorative opportunities. For example, it can be papered if the rest of the wall is plain, or painted using one of the special techniques explained on pages 50–75.

As these two rooms show, the waist-high dado rail is an effective way to divide a wall into different decorative areas.

Skirtingboard can range from a plain, wooden 'plank' to (as in some older houses) boards with 4–5in of decorative styling at the top. Not only does it protect the base of the wall from scuffs, knocks and run-away vacuum cleaners, but it also provides an opportunity for carved moulding. Most timber merchants and many DIY outlets carry a good range of skirtingboard, from simple to fancy.

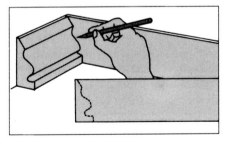

Mark outline of moulding on piece to be cut. Use a coping saw to cut out the outline of the moulding.

Architrave is the wooden moulding surrounding a door frame, and its simplicity or ornateness should be determined by the overall style of the room. It should be fixed to the door's subframe with countersunk nails and its corners mitred.

CORNERS

The technique of cutting decorative moulding for inside and outside corners is the same whether you are dealing with cornice, picture rails, dado or skirtingboard. Expanded polystyrene is much easier to handle than wooden moulding.

Inside corners Mark the contours of the moulding on to the edge of the length to be butted up and cut away the waste in order to make a neat fit, as the following diagrams show.

Outside corners Mitre the ends of the two pieces to be joined.

Put the moulding in a mitre box and cut the two pieces to be joined at a 45° angle.

Join the ends of the moulding with countersunk nails and neaten the outside join with filler compound if necessary.

FLOORS

SANDING FLOORS

The warm glow of stripped and sealed floorboards works well for both traditional and modern decors. The patina is a beautiful complement to antiques, while the simplicity is a counterfoil to the clean lines of modern furniture.

But the decision to expose floorboards is not just an aesthetic one; there are, in addition, some compelling cost considerations. For most people the highest decorating cost is likely to be laying fitted carpet, so the option of using floorboarding decoratively can be enticing. There are, though, a few points that ought to be borne in mind.

1. The gaps between boards can let in draughts. Much can be done to fill gaps (see below) and, of course, strategically placed rugs will help enormously to cut down on draughts. But serious gaps can only be dealt with adequately by lifting and relaying the boards – an extremely time-consuming and arduous job.

2. Bare boards will tend to make a room colder, irrespective of whether there are draughts or not. When thinking about stripping boards it is worth considering the aspect of the room. Is it south- or west-facing and therefore warmed by natural light which is highly flattering to the mellow tones of stripped wood? Or is it a north- or east-facing room in which the cold light will accentuate the bareness of the floor?

3. Bare floorboarding will amplify noise levels; where carpeting absorbs noise, floorboards reflect it. This is a consideration if you live in a flat where those who live below may be disturbed by increased noise.

4. Although a polyurethane varnish will afford good protection and wear well if enough coats are applied (three is a minimum), it will need to be rubbed down and reapplied periodically.

5. In older homes that have had a good bit of renovation work done over the years, the floorboarding may be unattractive. The boards may have been lifted, cut and relaid when electrical re-wiring or gas pipe-laying took place. When the boards are exposed you may find too many have been cut short, with ugly alignments of plank-ends. The floor might have an unattractive patched look rather than the elegant sleekness of long boards.

6. Sanding any significant area must be done with an industrial sanding machine. Painting and papering can be quite tranquil but sanding is unnervingly noisy and dusty. Most modern sanding machines have some kind of dust-collecting vacuum bag attached, but even so there will inevitably be a good deal of air-borne wood-dust. It is important to wear a dust mask and goggles because inhaling wood-dust can be hazardous and is also irritating to the eyes. Wearing ear mufflers is also recommended to cut down the effects of the very high noise levels of the sanding machine. Exposure to dust and noise for long periods is not only unhealthy but also very tiring. This is an important consideration when estimating how much time a job will take. On the one hand you will be anxious not to hire a sanding machine for longer than necessary, but it is much better to take your time and have frequent rest periods.

7. Handling big industrial floor sanders is strenuous work. They are powerful machines that need some strength to control properly. Again, do not plan to do too much at one go.

Above: *New floorboards offer a good smooth surface for floor stencilling.*
See pages 118 for techniques.

Left: *Wide floorboards usually date from the seventeenth or early eighteenth*
centuries. Here their natural beauty has been highlighted by sanding
(see pages 114–115) followed by a seal of several coats of polyurethane varnish
(see page 116).

SANDING EQUIPMENT

Most old floorboards will, over time, have become engrained with varnish, dirt, stains and grease. The surface has to be stripped back to clean wood before any finish can be applied. On large areas it is impractical to use hand-held sanders and the floor will first have to be scoured with a heavy-duty floor sander.

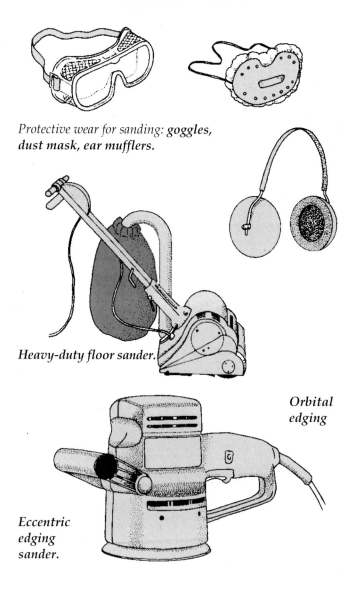

Protective wear for sanding: **goggles, dust mask, ear mufflers.**

Heavy-duty floor sander.

Eccentric edging sander.

FLOOR SANDERS

Industrial floor sanders are heavy and powerful tools. Most tool hire shops carry them, together with supplies of paper-backed abrasive belts (to be fitted to the sander's drum), goggles and face masks and ear mufflers. You will need three grades of abrasive belts: coarse to take off the worst of the surface and level the boards; medium and fine to smooth the boards ready for finishing. Make sure the hire shop either demonstrates how to fit the abrasive belts and operate the machine or gives you adequate written instructions. Most machines have a bar on the drum that is screwed down to secure the abrasive belt. It is important that the belt be neither too tight nor too loose. If too tight it will disintegrate on contact with the floor; if too loose, it may slip out and break up.

EDGING SANDERS

Big floor sanders cannot get right up to the edge of the boards, and this strip will have to be sanded with a smaller hand-held edging machine such as an orbital or 'eccentric' sander. These machines are not designed to strip deeply, as is the

Orbital edging

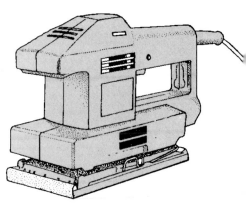

floor sander. The plate on an orbital sander oscillates in small circles at high speed (usually about 10,000 times a minute), so that the surface is left very smooth and with no scratches.

An eccentric sander not only oscillates like an orbital sander but also revolves, and is designed for edging work rather than heavy-duty sanding. The abrasive sheets are attached to the plate by Velcro, making for quick and easy replacement.

PREPARATION

The room should first be cleared of all furniture, curtains and, of course, any floorcovering. With the boarding now exposed, go over it carefully to find loose boards (nail them back to their joists) or protruding nail heads (hammer them back in and, if necessary, sink the heads below the surface with a counterpunch.) If the belt hits a raised nail head the belt can disintegrate with a loud bang; so time spent sinking nail heads will save frayed nerves as well as the cost of replacing abrasive belts.

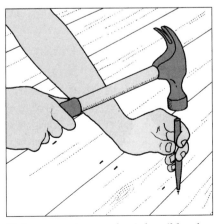

Using a counterpunch, sink nail heads below the surface.

If the gaps between the boards are more than about ⅛in (3mm) they should be filled to cut down on draughts. The best way to fill, and yet keep the natural look of the floor, is to hammer thin strips of wood into the gaps. This serves the additional function of tightening up the floor.

Cut a piece of thin lath and plane it until it fits very tightly into the gap but cannot be easily pushed all the way in. Coat both sides of the strip with wood adhesive.

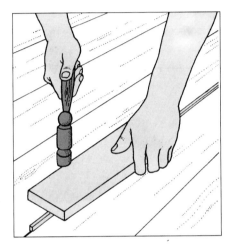

A block of wood protects the floor from hammer indents.

Place a block of wood over the strip and hammer on to that – it will protect the floor from becoming indented by the hammer.

If, after hammering, the strip still stands proud of the surface, plane it flush to the surrounding boards.

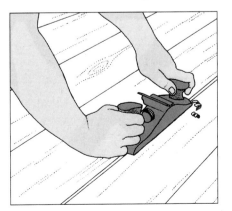

Planing the filling strip flush.

SANDING TECHNIQUE

Start by removing the surface of the boards with a heavy-duty floor sander fitted with the coarse abrasive belt. Begin with your back to the midpoint of a side wall and point the machine across the room to a diagonal corner. Holding the handle firmly with both hands, tilt the machine back on to its small rear

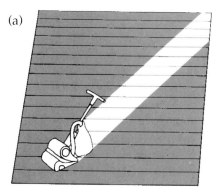

(a)

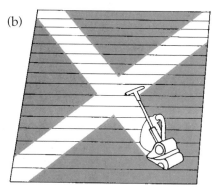

(b)

The sequence of sanding with a floor sander:
(a) across the first diagonal
(b) across the opposite diagonal
(c) up and down the boards.

(c)

wheels to lift the drum clear of the floor. Make sure that the electrical cord is out of the way (slinging it over your shoulder is a good solution). Switch on the machine and very gently lower the drum on to the floor. If you let it bang down there is a good chance that the abrasive belt will disintegrate.

A heavy-duty floor sander is powerful and will pull away as soon as the drum makes contact with the floor. Hold it back so that it travels slowly over the surface; but do not let it grind away on one spot for any time or it will wear a furrow in the wood. The machine is heavy, so you do not need to put any extra downward pressure on the drum. Keep it moving slowly and steadily across the floor.

Once the whole floor has been covered in one diagonal direction, repeat the process across the other diagonal, and then again up and down the length of the boards.

When you have thoroughly sanded with the coarse abrasive, sweep up loose dust (there will be a good deal, even though the machine is fitted with a vacuum bag), and repeat the whole process with medium-

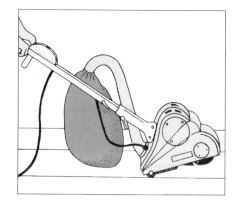

grade, and then fine-grade abrasive.

When you need a break, tilt the machine back on to its rear wheels and switch off. Do not lower the drum until it has come to a complete standstill. If there are children around, do not leave the sander unattended unless it has been disconnected at the plug.

If an abrasive belt breaks, switch off the machine and tilt it back only when the drum has stopped revolving. Do not change a belt without first having disconnected the machine at the plug.

Edging sanders do not need excessive downward pressure. There should be enough to prevent the plate skittering over the surface but not so much that the surface becomes scratched or scorched. Too much pressure will also clog the abrasive belts or discs. Keep the machine moving slowly and gently over the surface.

CORNERS

Neither floor nor edging sanders can get right into the corners, and this will have to be done with a hook-scraper followed by hand sanding with coarse, medium and fine sandpaper wrapped around a wood or cork sanding block.

CLEAN-UP

There will inevitably be a good deal of wood-dust to clean up – and not just from the floor. It is important to make sure that all surfaces, such as the tops of skirtingboards and door mouldings, are clean so that they cannot shed dust on to wet varnish.

Sweep up as much as you can, then hoover thoroughly. Finally wipe over the floor (and other surfaces) with a damp cloth and

Using a hook-scraper to get into the corners inaccessible to sanders.

Using an edging sander.

leave it to dry thoroughly before varnishing.

Remember that freshly sanded floors are particularly vulnerable to staining and marking before they have been sealed. Avoid walking over untreated surfaces in heavy shoes and, if necessary, protect the untreated surface with newspaper until you are ready to seal it.

FINISHING

Once the floor has been sanded, vacuumed, wiped over and allowed to dry, it is ready for finishing. There are several options, ranging from the simplest clear polyurethane varnish to painting and stencilling.

POLYURETHANE VARNISH

A classic finish is to simply brush the raw wood with several coats of polyurethane varnish (the first coat should be thinned with white spirit to act as a sealer). Not only is it hard-wearing, stain-resistant and heat-proof, clear polyurethane varnish will mellow the colour of the wood. Polurethane comes in matt, silk and gloss finishes, and it is really a matter of personal taste which you use. It is worth bearing in mind, though, that a high-gloss finish will tend to show scuffs and scratches more easily than a less shiny finish. It will also be more slippery.

You will need at least three coats of varnish, and preferably five, to give a truly hard-wearing seal. Apply the varnish with a brush (approximately 3in/75mm wide), and work it in down the length of the boards so that it penetrates the grain. Keep a lint-free rag dampened with a little white spirit to pick up anything that may fall into the varnish.

Allow each coat to dry (it takes about 12 hours usually, but the time will vary according to the humidity and temperature of the atmosphere) and then rub the surface down with medium sandpaper followed by a wipe over with a rag dampened with

Brush the polyurethane varnish along the grain, not across.

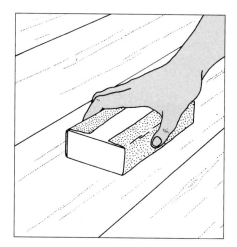

Rub down each coat of varnish with medium sandpaper to give a key for the next coat. Wipe up the dust before applying the next coat.

white spirit before applying the next coat. You will not need to rub down the final coat.

A polyurethane finish should last at least two years of normal wear. When it needs to be freshened up, rub it down with medium and then fine sandpaper, wipe over with a tack rag and, when dry, brush on one or two coats of polyurethane.

Good-quality acrylic varnish is now available which, because it is faster drying than conventional polyurethane varnish, allows up to three coats to be applied in one day.

WOOD STAINS

One of the ways to change the colour of floorboarding is with wood stains. There is a wide range of colours to choose from that not only encompasses natural wood colours from pale ash to dark mahogany but also other colours such as blue, green, red etc. Acrylic stains in satin finish (in a range of wood tones) colour and protect wood.

A wider range of colours are found in water- or oil-based stains, and of these the oil-based version is probably preferable. It will dry more slowly than water-based stain and is therefore less likely to dry patchily.

Stains can be brushed on, or rubbed on with a lint-free cloth. The wood must first be sanded and wiped over to remove any remaining dust. Apply the stain until you have the density of colour you want and, when the stain has completely dried, give it at least three coats of clear polyurethane varnish. The varnish will tend to darken the colour of the stain a little, so it is best to experiment on a spare piece of board.

LIGHTENING

Most floorboarding will be of deal or pine, both of which occasionally turn a rather unattractive raw orangey-red if just simply varnished. This can be toned down with white, oil-based undercoat to which has been added a squirt of raw umber and black artists' colours (bought by the tube at artists' materials suppliers). Mix the paint well to get an even distribution of the artists' colours.

The boards should be sanded in the usual way (see pages 108–115) and cleaned of all dust. Using a stiff-bristled brush (a small scrubbing brush would do) work the paint well into the grain without putting on too thick a coat. Work on smallish sections at a time, say 3ft (1m) x 3ft (1m). While the paint is still wet, take a lint-free cloth and rub across the grain to remove some of the paint. Switch to clean cloths as the used ones become soaked in paint. Allow the paint to dry thoroughly before sealing it with at least three coats of clear polyurethane varnish.

PAINTED FLOORS

An increasingly popular alternative to transparent varnishing is to paint sanded floorboards. Any kind of paint can be used because it will be protected by several coats of clear polyurethane varnish.

Once the floor has been sanded and prepared in the usual way (see pages 108-115), it will need to be primed with all-purpose primer and a coat or two of undercoat. It can then be painted with oil- or water-based paint. When the final paint finish is dry, apply at least three coats of clear polyurethane varnish.

STENCILLED FLOORS

In essence, the technique for stencilling a floor is no different from that used to stencil walls (see pages 69–71). However, stencilling is best done on boards that are not too badly ridged and uneven. Using hardboard squares offers a good stencilling surface if the floorboarding is unacceptable (see next page).

It is a good idea to plan the stencil pattern in miniature on squared paper, starting at the centre of the room and marking off squares to represent the pattern repeats.

Planning

When it comes to transferring the design to the floor, the first job is to locate the centre point of the room.

Find the mid-points of opposite walls and fix a length of chalked string from one to the other. Pull the string tight and draw it back like a bowstring; let it snap on to the floor to leave a chalk line. Repeat this process with the two opposite walls. The centre point of the room is where the chalk lines intersect. Mark off these lines in the size squares you want.

Taking the last points before the walls use a try-square to mark lines at right-angles to the main axes and likewise mark off these lines into squares. You will now have axes and sidelines marked off. Now taking the last points before the top and bottom walls, make right-angles and join the sidelines at top and bottom. Now you have the whole perimeter marked out and squared-off. It only remains to join points from opposite sidelines and top/bottom lines to square-off the whole floor (see diagram on facing page).

Careful measurement is important when squaring-off as small errors at the beginning will become magnified as the job proceeds.

Techniques

The kinds of paint used for floor stencils are much the same as for stencilled walls (see page 69), as too are the basic techniques of applying the stencils and paint.

Floor stencils are often less delicately patterned than those used on walls, so the largest-size stencil brush or even a 1-2in (25–50mm) paint brush used with a stippling stroke will cover the larger area more quickly. Aerosol paints can cover large areas quickly, but they have a couple of disadvantages. When an aerosol is pointed straight down, the nozzle tends to clog quickly, which means time lost cleaning it. When pointed at an angle to avoid clogging, the paint is often forced under the stencil, spoiling the outline (scoring round the stencil outline with an awl or Stanley knife can help minimise this problem).

Floor stencilling tends to be less precise than wall stencilling (partly because of the greater area to be covered and the strain of bending over the stencil makes you tired and prone to the odd lapse) and you will probably find runs and smudges under the stencil. Wipe them up with a cloth dampened in the appropriate solvent (water for water-based paints such as emulsion or acrylics; white spirit for oils) and keep the back of the stencil clean.

Allow the stencilled pattern to dry completely before protecting the whole floor with at least three coats of clear polyurethane varnish.

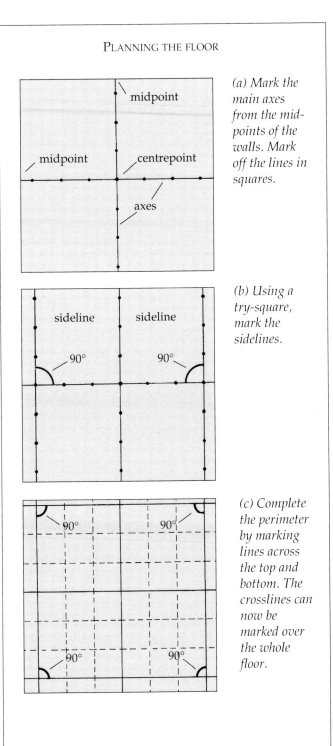

PLANNING THE FLOOR

(a) Mark the main axes from the midpoints of the walls. Mark off the lines in squares.

(b) Using a try-square, mark the sidelines.

(c) Complete the perimeter by marking lines across the top and bottom. The crosslines can now be marked over the whole floor.

HARDBOARD FLOORING

If the floorboarding is too badly damaged to expose, or if there are large gaps, an alternative is to cover the floor with squares of hardboard. Plain hardboard is not particularly attractive, but it makes an excellent base for painting and stencilling, either using the natural brown as a background colour or painting on a base colour.

The large hardboard sheets need to be cut into more manageable squares of about 2ft (60cm) x 2ft (60cm). Sometimes a timber supplier will do this for you, or you can do it at home using an electric jigsaw or hand panel saw.

You can stencil or paint the individual squares (on the smooth side) at this stage if you wish, or after you have laid them.

The hardboard must be cured so that it does not absorb moisture from the atmosphere and buckle after it has been laid. Sponge water on to the back (rough) side of each square and let it dry out. Keep the squares stacked and weighted until the hardboard is dry. Glue and/or tack the squares to the floor, making sure they butt up tightly to one another.

If you intend to paint or stencil the hardboard (and do not want to use the natural brown as background colour), seal it first with a thinned coat of sealer and one or two coats of emulsion or oil-based undercoat.

Whether painted or stencilled, the hardboard will have to be protected with at least three coats of clear polyurethane varnish.

FLOOR TILES

Floor tiles come in a wide variety of materials, shapes, sizes and finishes. They are probably one of the most durable of floorcoverings and range in price from expensive ceramics right down to cheap vinyl tiles.

It is worth taking time to gather samples and see what they look like *in situ*. If you make a mistake with carpeting it will certainly be expensive to replace it, but at least it is relatively easy to do. Taking up tiling is a good deal messier and time consuming.

Consider which of the main two types of tile – 'hard' or 'soft' – is going to be best. The soft tiles include cork, vinyl and rubber. Hard tiles include ceramic, slate and quarry. Apart from purely aesthetic considerations, weigh up the practical advantages and disadvantages:
* Soft tiles are warmer, more comfortable to the feet, generally cheaper and easier to lay than hard tiles. They also provide better sound-proofing than hard tiles.
* Hard tiles are stylish, extremely hard wearing and easy to maintain. They can be tricky to lay in a space with lots of corners and angles because they are difficult to cut with the same precision as soft tiling.

HARD FLOOR TILES

Hard floor tiles are usually a good deal thicker than wall tiles. After all, they have considerable loads to bear – weights and stresses that would crack most wall tiles if they were used on the floor.

Hard floor tiles come in a wide range of shapes, colours and finishes. To some extent the old distinction between indoor and outdoor tiles has been blurred. Traditional outdoor tiles such as quarry and slate are now firmly established indoors. As some of these outdoor tiles are porous and would quickly absorb spills and stains they should be sealed with a proprietary tile sealant or two coats of linseed oil diluted by 50% with white spirit. It is not advisable to use interior tiles for outdoor use unless you know they are frost-proof, otherwise they will soon fracture.

Preparing the underfloor

Hard floor tiles need to be laid on to a solid base that is flat, clean and dry. Laying straight on to floorboarding is not recommended because even the slightest unevenness will cause tiles to rock and eventually dislodge. Cover the floor with plywood sheets that have been nailed and glued to the floorboarding. Hardboard sheets are probably an adequate base for soft tiles, but not for hard. Professionals recommend that the combined thickness of floorboarding and plywood be at least 1¼in (31mm). Lay the plywood panels in a staggered pattern to prevent long runs of aligned edges, and leave a slight gap (about ¹⁄₁₆in/2mm) to allow for any expansion. Seal the plywood with either a thin coat of adhesive or a sealant recommended by the manufacturer.

Concrete floors must be completely dry. Check for dampness by taping several squares of clear plastic (shrink-wrap, for example) to the concrete and leave them for 24 hours. If the squares become misted on the underside, you have a damp problem that will have to be cured before you lay the tiles. The surface

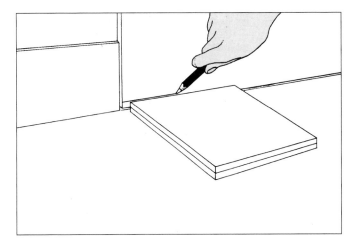

must also be flat, and free of grease and dust.

Adhesives

The tile supplier's advice and the tile manufacturer's instructions are the best guide to choosing the appropriate adhesive and the thickness you will need to properly bed the tile. If you are working in an area that is likely to get wet (a shower or entrance hall, for example) you will need an adhesive that is waterproof once it has dried.

When you are laying tiles on to floorboards (even though they will be covered with sheets of plywood) you will probably need a rubber-based adhesive that has enough flexibility to accommodate the natural spring of a wooden floor. If hot water or central-heating pipes or elements run under the floor, choose a heat-resistant adhesive.

The quick-set adhesives now available mean that tiles can be laid, grouted and walked on in the same day. Most adhesives come with a notched comb spreader but a little extra spent on a notched trowel will speed up the the work and create a better bed for the tiles.

Preparation

Before you start, check the boxes of tiles for colour variations and make sure you have the appropriate adhesive and grout. You may also need to check that doors opening into the room will be able to clear the tiles. Put two tiles, one on the other, up against the door and, if necessary, mark the bottom of the door where it will need to be cut.

Marking out the floor

There are basically two ways of planning out the floor: working out from the walls or working from the centre of the room. Whichever you choose, the aim is to plan the tiling so that you avoid having to use very narrow edging pieces. It is difficult to cut less than 2in (50mm) from thinner ceramic tiles with any accuracy and neatness. With thick tiles such as quarry, you should aim to edge with half-width tiles. You should also plan to have equal-width edging on opposite ends of the row, otherwise you will end up with a lopsided effect.

A useful and simple tool to help mark out the floor is a batten (about 4ft/1.2m) marked off in sections equal to the width of the tile plus the grouting gaps between the tiles.

Marking the door to be cut for clearance.

Marking off a measuring batten.

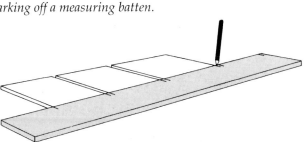

Working from walls

1. Using the measuring batten (or simply laying down loose tiles) calculate how many whole tiles will be needed across the floor. Place the batten or first tile hard up against one wall and continue across the room.

2. Assuming there is not an exact fit, you will be left with a gap at the end of the row. Divide this gap by two and measure out this distance from the wall. This will ensure that an edge of equal width will be left at the other end of the row when you come to lay the tiles permanently.

3. Repeat this process across the other dimension of the floor and mark in from the adjacent wall.

4. Working from one corner, tack a batten along the edging line of one wall. Align the adjacent batten along its edging line and butt it up to the

Laying the first batten. Make sure the battens form a right angle.

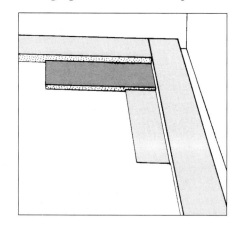

first batten to make a right-angle. It is important that the two battens form a true right-angle because the first tile will determine the alignment of the rest of the tiles, so check the junction of the battens with a try-square.

5. Starting in the corner, spread the adhesive to cover an area of about 3ft (1m) x 3ft (1m).

Spreading the first batch of adhesive into the corner.

6. Lay the first tile in the corner formed by the battens and make sure it butts firmly against both.

7. Continue to lay tiles along one batten, ensuring they butt up to the batten. Separate each tile with spacers (unless the tiles already have spacing lugs along their sides) to allow for grouting. Continue to the edge of the adhesive.

8. Return to the beginning of the first row and start to lay the second alongside, making sure the first tile butts up firmly to the batten.

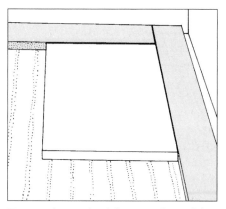

Ensure that each of the two edges of the tile in contact with the battens butt up tightly.

Working from the centre

1. Measure along two opposite walls and tack nails into the floor at the walls' midpoints. Stretch chalked string tightly between the nails.

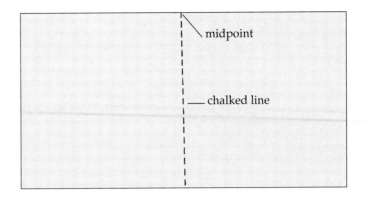

2. Starting at the midpoint of the string, lay a loose tile at right-angles to the string. Carry on laying loose tiles in a row (allowing space between each for grouting) until you reach the far wall. If the space between the last tile and the wall is less than about 3in (75mm) move the whole row back to give an edging gap of about 3in (75mm). Reset the nails and string by the distance you have moved the tiles. Snap the string against the floor to give you a chalk guideline.

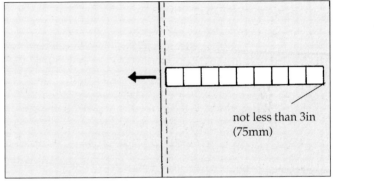

3. Stretch a second chalked string between the midpoints of the remaining two walls. Lay a row of loose tiles at right-angles to the first. If the gap between the last tile and the wall is less than about 3in (75mm) move both the second row and the first back until you have an edging gap of about 3in (75mm). Reposition the string by the distance you have moved the tiles and snap a second chalk guideline on to the floor.

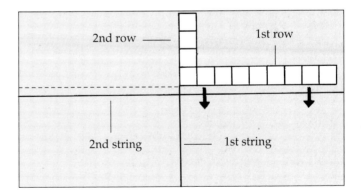

Laying tiles

Work out from the centre, a quadrant at a time. Spread enough adhesive to cover an area of about nine tiles (without obliterating the chalk line with adhesive).

Fit the first tile so that two edges align with the chalk lines and continue to lay the tiles in 'pyramid' fashion.

Work from the centre of one quadrant, laying the tiles in pyramid fashion.

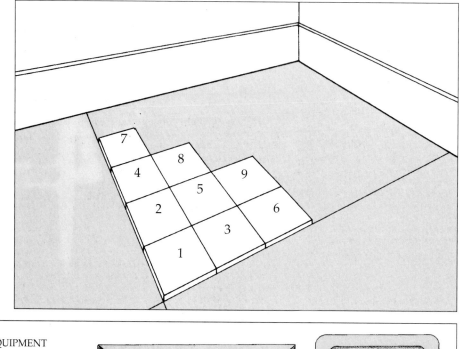

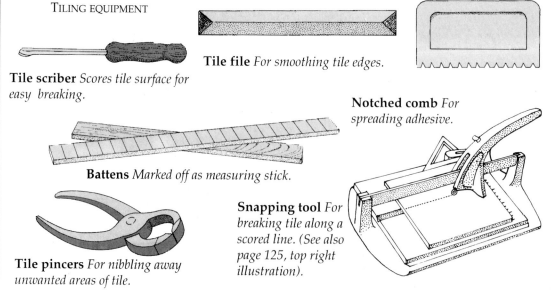

TILING EQUIPMENT

Tile scriber *Scores tile surface for easy breaking.*

Tile file *For smoothing tile edges.*

Notched comb *For spreading adhesive.*

Battens *Marked off as measuring stick.*

Snapping tool *For breaking tile along a scored line. (See also page 125, top right illustration).*

Tile pincers *For nibbling away unwanted areas of tile.*

Cutting edging tiles

Because most rooms are out of square, you will almost certainly have to cut edging tiles to fit. A tungsten-blade tile saw is very useful for complicated shapes, but the following method is a quick and easy way of cutting edging tiles:

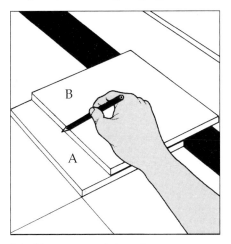

Marking out an edging tile.

1. Lay a dry tile (A) exactly over the last full tile before the wall. Place another dry tile (B) on top of (A) and slide it up until it butts up to the wall or skirtingboard. Mark tile (A) along the edge of tile (B).

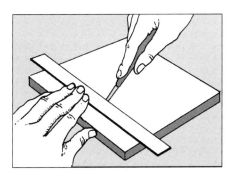

2. Add ⅛in (3mm) for grouting and score along the line with a tile cutter (again inexpensive and widely available from DIY outlets and tile suppliers).

Centre the tile cutting tool on the scored line.

3. Either use a special tile-breaking tool (inexpensive and widely available) (1) or break the tile across a thin piece of wood (2).

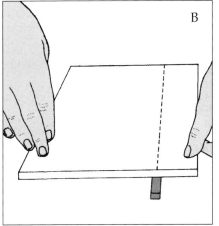

Breaking the tile over a thin piece of wood.

4. In order to get a clean break, make sure the surface of the tile has been scored deeply enough to cut through the glaze. When you come to snap the tile, ensure that the scored line is directly over the piece of wood or tile, or that the tile-breaking tool is centred on the scored line.

Corner tiles

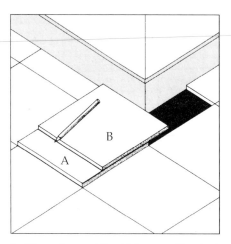

1. Place loose tile (A) over the last whole tile before the corner so that it covers it exactly. Place tile (B) on to tile (A) and slide it so that one edge butts the wall or skirtingboard. Mark tile (A) along the inward edge of tile (B).

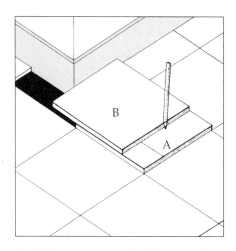

2. Without turning tile (A) move it to the other side of the corner and place it over the last full tile before the corner, covering it exactly. Place tile (B) on top and slide (B) until it butts up against the wall or skirtingboard. Mark (A) along the inward edge of (B). This second line will intersect the first.

3. Having allowed for the grouting gap, score the lines with a tile cutter.

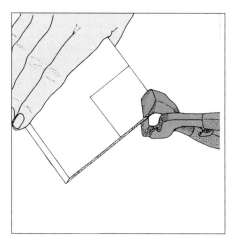

4. The area of tile to be removed will have to be nibbled away with tile pincers.

Grouting

Grouting (the filler used between tiles) can be bought ready-mixed or in powder form to be mixed with water according to the manufacturer's instructions.

1. Do not grout until the tile adhesive has dried thoroughly. Remove any spacers if they stand proud of the surface of the tile; leave them in if they are sunk below surface level.

2. Work in small areas at a time (about 3ft/1m x 3ft/1m) and spread the grout over the tiles with a rubber grouting tool (the spring in the rubber is useful for getting the grout well down into the joints).

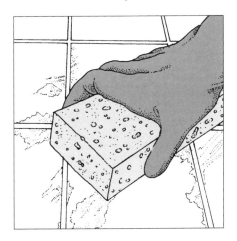

3. Wipe off the excess grout with a wet sponge as you go.

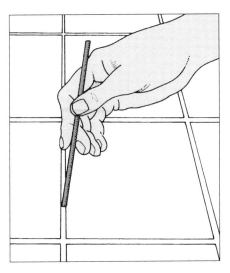

4. Run a piece of dowel (about as thick as a pencil) along the joints. Alternatively you could run a finger down the joints, but as grouting sometimes contains chemicals that can irritate the skin wear rubber gloves.

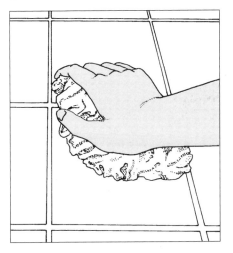

5. Wipe off any streaks and smears left by dry grout with a dry, soft cloth and buff up the tile surface.

CUTTING QUARRY TILES

The thickness of quarry tiles makes them difficult to snap in the way you would an ordinary ceramic tile. Score the face of the quarry tile in the normal way using a tile cutter. Wearing gloves, turn the tile over and, holding it firmly, strike it smartly beneath the scored line.

The L-shape of a corner tile should be nibbled with tile pincers in much the same way you would with a ceramic tile.

But this can be made much easier if first you use a hammer to chip away at the back of the area to be removed in order to reduce the tile's thickness at that point.

Breaking a quarry tile.

Thinning the back of a quarry tile before nibbling the waste area with tile pincers.

SOFT TILES

Soft tiles such as vinyl, cork and rubber, have the great advantage of being easy to cut and shape. A good sharp Stanley knife is really all you need.

As with hard tiles, though, you will need a solid, smooth, clean and dry sub-floor on which to lay the tiles. Floorboards should be covered with sheets of plywood or hardboard (with their edges staggered as described on page 120), nailed and glued. If you use hardboard, cure it by brushing the back (rough side) of each sheet with water. Leave the sheets stacked back-to-back for at least 24 hours to let them adjust to the humidity of the room in which they will be laid. Leave a slight gap between sheets (about ⅛in/3mm) for expansion.

The planning of the floor is essentially no different from the techniques for laying hard tiles (see page 121). However, soft tiles, being larger in area than hard tiles, are probably best laid from the centre of the room (see page 123).

The technique for cutting edging and corner tiles is, again, the same as described on pages 125-126. (However, you will need to use a Stanley knife to cut the tiles).

Tricky shapes, such as those around the mouldings of door frames or the base of a lavatory can be dealt with either by making a paper template or by using a profile gauge (see facing page). The pins of the gauge, when pressed up against the moulding, will conform to its outline. The pins are then locked in place and the shape traced off on to the tile.

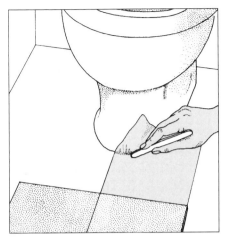

1. Using a paper template the same size as a tile, offer it up and crease it around the base of the lavatory.

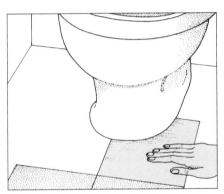

2. Having cut round the crease, check the template for fit.

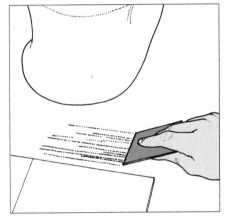

3. Mark the tile to be fitted, cut it and fit it (making minor adjustments as necessary). Repeat each of the steps for the rest of the lavatory base.

4. Cutting the marked-out tile.

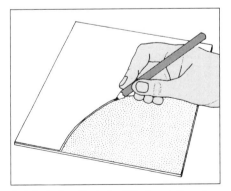

5. Spreading adhesive on the sub-floor.

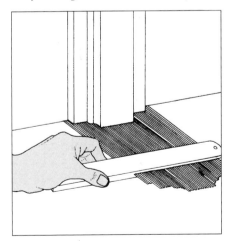

Using a profile gauge around a door frame.

TILING WALLS

CERAMIC TILES

Generally lighter and thinner than floor tiles, ceramic wall tiles are correspondingly easier to cut and shape. 'Field' tiles will be used in most of the area to be tiled. Field tiles are squared off on all four edges. Some tiles have lugs on their edges which act as spacers; others (called universal tiles) have bevelled edges that ensure automatic spacing. If the tiles you choose are not universal or lugged they will need to be separated from each other by spacers to allow a gap for grouting. Purpose-made plastic spacers can be bought from DIY outlets and tile suppliers, or you can use small nails or even matchsticks as spacers.

PREPARATION

As with floor tiles, wall tiles must be fixed to a rigid, smooth, dry and clean surface. Do not tile over wall-covering.

If the wall is new plaster, make sure it is perfectly dry and has been sealed with primer-sealer. If the wall has been previously painted with gloss, rub it down with coarse sand-paper to give a key for the tile adhesive.

Emulsioned walls need no special preparation but ensure the surface is dust- and grease-free. Wash down with a solution of warm water and a little washing-up liquid followed by a wash-down with clean water. Allow the surface to dry completely. Fill larger cracks and holes. If the wall is uneven, the tiles may rock and dislodge.

Remove as many fittings (towel rails, etc) as you can. If possible, loosen light switch covers (having first turned off the electricity). It is much easier to tile behind the switch cover and then tighten it up flush to the tile than it is to tile round it.

PLANNING

The objective is no different to tiling a floor. You will almost certainly have to cut tiles to fill edging gaps, and you should plan to have them in inside corners or at ceiling height where they will be less conspicuous.

OTHER WALL TILES

Cork. Most are 12in (300mm) sq and about ⅛in (3mm) thick. Set them out on true vertical and horizontal guidelines, although support battens are not necessary. Adhesive recommended by the manufacturer should be spread on the wall and tile back and left for the specified time. For cutting see pages 128-129.

Mirror. Usually 6 x 9in (150 x 225mm), mirror tiles come in bronze, silver and smoke-grey finishes. They are fixed to the wall with the adhesive pads on the back of the tile. Any surface unevenness will cause a distorted image. Cut by scoring with a glass-cutter and snapping with a tile-breaker (see page 125).

Metallic. This sheet metal tiles comes in 4½, 6, 12in sq (112, 150, 300mm sq) sizes and a range of metallic colours, sheens and decorative patterns. They are fixed to the wall by pads, like mirror tiles, but because they are less reflective than mirror tiles they do not show up surface irregularities as much. Cut with scissors or tin-snips. To bend, nick the edges of the tile at the end of the bend line and gently bend the tile around the edge of a wood block.
As with all tiles, buy about 5% more than you strictly need. Buying replacement tiles that match the originals may be difficult.

If a window or windows break up the wall these will be the focal point and you should plan to have whole tiles or at least equal-sized cut tiles around the edge of the windows.

A measuring batten like the one described on page 121 (but, of course, marked out for wall tiles plus space for grouting gaps) will speed up the planning process.

FIRST STEP: THE HORIZONTAL LINE

Skirtingboards and floors may not be truly horizontal and to use them as the guideline for the first row of tiles would probably end up in some very skewed tiling. The first job is to fix a batten at the foot of the wall which is truly horizontal and on which the first row of tiles will sit.

Find the lowest level of the top of the skirtingboard or floor (if there is no skirtingboard) by setting a spirit level at various points. Put a loose tile at that point and set the spirit level on it. Draw a light horizontal pencil line ⅛in (2mm) above the tile (to allow for grouting).

Using a measuring batten or straightedge, measure the distance from the horizontal line to the ceiling (or cornice, if that is where the tiling will end). If you find you are left with a gap at the top of less than 2in (50mm), drop the horizontal line to give you about a half-tile gap at top and bottom. Although it always looks nicer to have a row of full tiles at the bottom, the guiding principle is symmetry.

Once you have established the position of the footing horizontal, mark it off in pencil and continue it across the wall and round on to any other walls that you intend to tile.

Take a batten (or battens if necessary) and nail or screw them to

the wall so that the top edge of the batten sits exactly on the pencil line. To a large extent the look of the whole job will be determined by the care taken in making sure the footing battens are exactly horizontal.

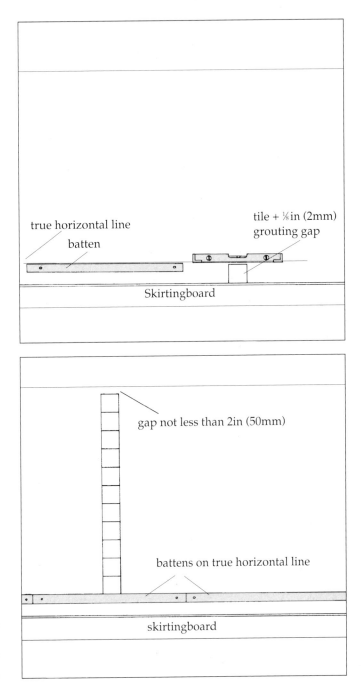

true horizontal line

batten

tile + ⅛in (2mm) grouting gap

Skirtingboard

gap not less than 2in (50mm)

battens on true horizontal line

skirtingboard

SECOND STEP: THE VERTICAL LINE

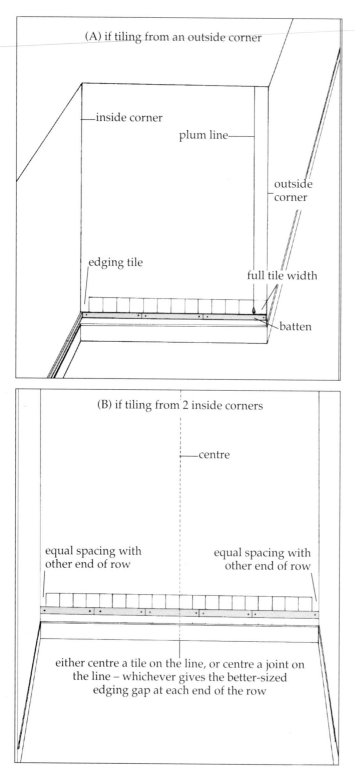

(A) if tiling from an outside corner

inside corner

plum line

outside corner

edging tile

full tile width

batten

(B) if tiling from 2 inside corners

centre

equal spacing with other end of row

equal spacing with other end of row

either centre a tile on the line, or centre a joint on the line – whichever gives the better-sized edging gap at each end of the row

Again, the aim is to plan the tiling so that cut tiles are placed as inconspicuously as possible at an inside corner.

If the wall has an outside corner (see illustration A) start with whole tiles there. Snap a plumb line (see page 88) or use a spirit level to mark a vertical line one tile (plus grouting gap) in from the outside corner. Plan to tile across towards the inside corner, using the cut tiles to fill the gap there if necessary.

If the wall has two inside corners (see illustration B) mark a vertical line at the midpoint of the wall. Using the measuring batten, or by laying loose tiles (allowing for grouting gaps between them) along the footing batten, you will be able to see what gap is left at the inside corner. Plan the first tile so that the centre vertical line either runs through the centre of the tile, or through the joint between two tiles – whichever gives a better-sized edging tile at the end. Try to avoid an edging tile of less than 2in (50mm) if possible.

TILING SEQUENCE

Start tiling from the footing batten upwards. Apply the adhesive with a comb applicator (similar to that shown on page 124). Do not slide the tiles in the adhesive as this will

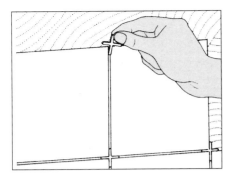

Purpose-made plastic spacers.

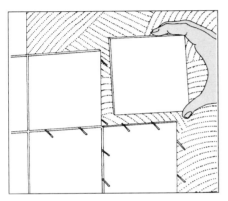

Using small nails as spacers.

merely push the adhesive into the joints. Give each tile a little twist as you align it in order to seat it in the adhesive securely.

If the tile is not self-spacing (i.e. does not have lugs on its edges or is bevelled for automatic spacing) put spacers (either small nails lightly tacked into the wall or purpose-made plastic cruciform spacers) between the tiles.

As the rows begin to build, check them for horizontal alignment with a spirit level.

Tiling sequence for half walls

If you are planning to tile part way up a wall, say to waist level, mark a true horizontal at the upper point and plan to finish there with full tiles. Adjust the footing batten accordingly and fill below it with cut tiles.

CUTTING TILES

Inside corners

When it comes to filling edging gaps, take a whole loose tile (A) and place it, glazed face to the wall, over the last full tile (B) before the gap to be filled. The back of the tile to be cut is now facing you. Slide tile (A) until its edge butts up against the adjacent wall.

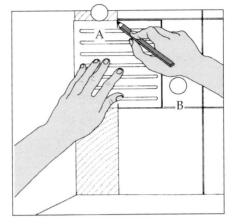

Use a pencil to mark on the back of tile (A) where it meets the edge of tile (B). Add an extra ⅛in (2mm) for grouting between the tiles. Carry this line around on to the glazed face of tile (A) and score it with a tile cutter. The tile can now be broken as described on page 125. If the gap is too narrow to use the adhesive applicator, apply the adhesive to the back of the edging tile. The cut edge of the tile will go into the corner, leaving the neater and more visible edge butting tile (B).

Outside corners

Outside corners should have the edge of the regular field tile covered by the rounded edge of a purpose-made edging tile on the adjacent wall. Universal tiles have bevelled edges that make neat joins at outside corners without having to use special edging tiles.

AWKWARD SPACES

For cutting L-shaped tiles see page 126. For tiles that need a curve (for example round the bowl of a hand basin) use a paper template as described on page 129.

CUTTING AROUND PIPES

Mark the centre of the pipe on the edge of a loose tile and cut the tile into two pieces at that point. Offer up each piece of the tile (cut edge to the pipe) and mark the diameter of the pipe on the tile. Nip away the area to be removed with tile pincers (see page 126). Apply the adhesive to the back of each piece of tile and stick them in place.

Marking-off the diameter of the pipe.

Fitting-up the cut tile.

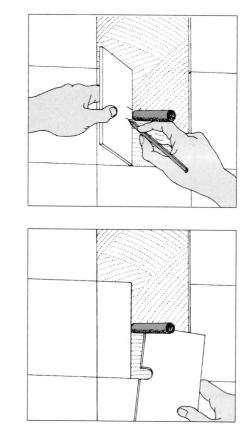

RECESSED WINDOWS

If you plan to tile into a window recess put full tiles at the outer edge of the recess and fill in the gap at the back of the recess with cut tiles where they will be less noticeable.

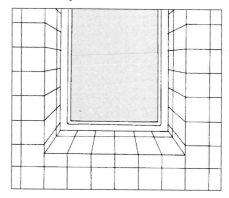

Plan for whole tiles at the outer edge of a recessed window.

The whole tiles on the outer edge of the recess should be special edging tiles with one rounded edge (unless you are using universal tiles which will automatically make a neat butt). The special edging tiles should protrude from the recess just enough to cover the flat edge of the tiles on the adjoining wall.

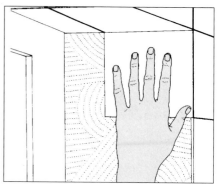

The tile inside the recess should have a rounded edge that will cover the edge of the tile on the adjoining wall.

FIXING ACCESSORIES

Many accessories, such as soap dishes and toothbrush holders, are available in ceramic which matches the surrounding tiling. Once the accessory has been backed with adhesive, it should be stuck into the space in the tiling left for it and held in place with masking tape until the adhesive has set (about 24 hours).

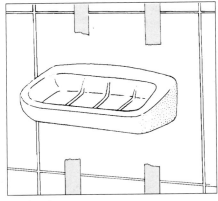

Taping in an accessory.

If you need to screw accessories into the tiles, aim to drill the screw holes as close to the centre of the tiles as possible. This will reduce the possibility of cracking the tile. A masonry drill bit will skid over the glazed surface of a tile, so first cover the spot to be drilled with masking tape to give the drill some purchase.

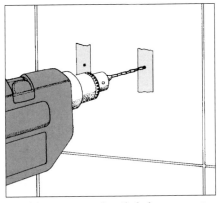

Masking tape on the tile helps prevent the drill bit from slipping.

GROUTING

Grout is a type of filler compound that can be bought either ready-mixed or in powder form to be mixed with water (according to the manufacturer's instructions.) Use waterproof grout where necessary. Coloured grouts are also available to match a wide range of coloured tiles.

Before grouting, the adhesive should be thoroughly dry. This usually takes about 24 hours, but temperature and humidity can either advance or retard drying time. Follow the manufacturer's instructions.

The easiest way to apply grout is with a rubber-faced trowel or with the spreader shown on page 127.

While the grout is still wet, wipe the surface with a damp sponge to push the grout well into the joints.

Before the grout dries, run a thin piece of dowel or the back of an old toothbrush, for example, along the joints to get a neat finish. Finally, wipe any excess grout from the face of the tiles with a damp sponge and polish the tiles with a soft cloth.

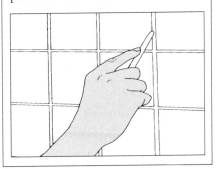

PAINTING EXTERIORS

Although the prospect of repairing and painting the outside of our homes is not exactly thrilling, we know that it is probably the single most important thing we can do to protect our investment.

External faults, if neglected, can lead to serious damage from rot and damp that will not only undermine the fabric of the building but can also ruin interior and exterior decoration.

Priority should be given to any repair that helps keep the structure watertight. And if you have decided to repaint the outside of your home, then this is also the time to make a comprehensive survey of all potential repairs as well as existing paintwork.

Although the following checklist includes some structural elements that are not strictly to do with painting, the time to take care of them is before, not after, you have finished painting. Unless underlying problems are sorted out, a new paint job is a waste of time.

TOUR OF INSPECTION

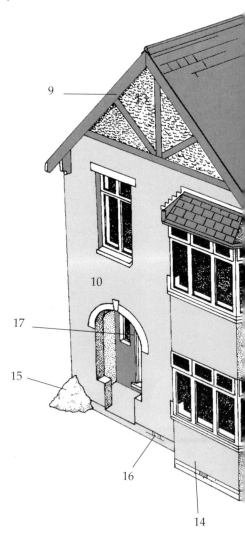

1. **The Roof.** Inspect the whole roof for loose and damaged slates and tiles (a pair of binoculars is helpful if you do not want to clamber over the roof itself). After a period of rain go into the loft and inspect for damp. Check the roofing battens for softness caused by wet rot.

2. **Loft Ventilation.** Without adequate ventilation in the loft space, condensation can form which may lead to rot. Ventilation can be provided by air bricks in gable walls or by special ventilating slates or tiles. Holes (about 2in/50mm across) can also be drilled at 8in (200mm) intervals in the boards under the eaves. Cover them with wire mesh to prevent pigeons and other unwelcome guests getting in.

3. **Chimney.** Look for damaged flashings (4), the seals that waterproof joints. Minor DIY repairs can be made using flashing tape, but more extensive repair should be carried out professionally. Check the flaunching (5) that holds the chimney in place, and make sure the mortar on the chimney stack is solid.

6. **Gutters and Downpipes.** Leaks are obviously more noticeable during a downpour but a bucket of water poured into the gutter furthest away from the downpipe will also highlight problems. If iron guttering and pipes are badly rusted they should be replaced with plastic.

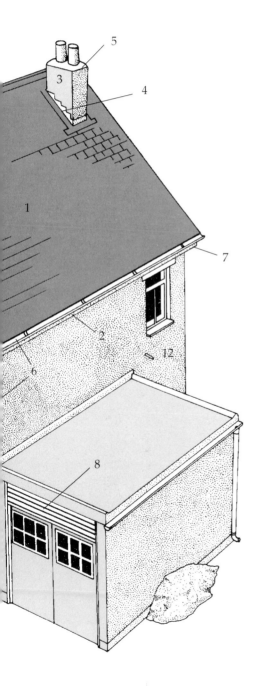

7. **Fascia Boards.** These are the boards to which guttering is attached. Prod with a screwdriver to test if they are soft and rotted. This screwdriver test should be used on all exterior wood: window frames, doors, cladding (8) and barge boards (9).

10. **Walls.** Check for mould and algae growth (11), particularly behind gutters and downpipes (see page 149 for remedies). If the overflow pipe (12) is leaking it may leave water stains on new paintwork (check the tank). Look at rendering and pebbledash (13) for cracks that can trap water. Check the pointing (the mortar joins between bricks) and have it professionally repointed if damage is extensive. If it is a small area, you can probably tackle it yourself with a small trowel and ready-mixed mortar, having first raked out the crumbly old mortar.

14. The damp-proof course (DPC) is usually about two bricks up from the ground and will look like a thicker line of mortar, perhaps with the edge of the black membrane (usually bituminous felt or PVC) showing through. Older houses may have slate or lead DPCs, or sometimes just two courses of dense bricks which may have been replaced by a chemically injected DPC (look for tell-tale holes). It is important that the DPC has not been breached at any point, or ground moisture will rise into the walls. This may happen, for example, when piles of rubble or earth (15) are left against a wall. This effectively short-circuits the DPC. Ensure that the ground level is about 6in (150mm) below the DPC.

16. **Airbricks.** Clear the holes to ensure a good flow of air under the floorboards.

17. **Windows and Doors.** Use the screwdriver test to check for wet rot. Make sure the groove that runs under window sills is not blocked with old paint or dirt. Check the puttying around panes, and for gaps between door and window frames and the surrounding walls. For other problems on walls and woodwork, see page 148-149.

EXTERIOR EQUIPMENT

Although most of us will only have to redecorate the outside of our houses about every 4-6 years (if you live by the sea or in a particularly exposed location, it will almost certainly be more often) it is worth buying sturdy, quality tools. Not only do they make the job easier because they perform more efficiently than their cheaper counterparts, but they usually turn out to be more economical in the longer run. If they are cleaned and stored properly (see pages 48-49) good tools will last through many redecorations.

In addition to the smaller tools shown here (which you would almost certainly want to buy) there are larger items such as ladders (see pages 142-145), access towers (see pages 146-147) and paint sprayers (see pages 153-155) that it is probably more economical to hire.

EQUIPMENT FOR PREPARATION

Hot-air stripper *For removing paint from woodwork.*

Putty knife.

Scraper *For lifting paint from flat areas of woodwork and walls.*

Shavehook *For removing paint from wood mouldings.*

Small trowel *For repointing and filling cracks and small holes in masonry.*

Filling knife.

Electric drill *and* **wire-brush attachments** *For removing rust from metalwork.*

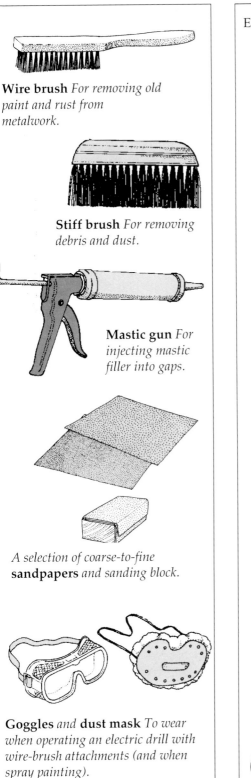

Wire brush *For removing old paint and rust from metalwork.*

Stiff brush *For removing debris and dust.*

Mastic gun *For injecting mastic filler into gaps.*

A selection of coarse-to-fine **sandpapers** *and sanding block.*

Goggles *and* **dust mask** *To wear when operating an electric drill with wire-brush attachments (and when spray painting).*

EQUIPMENT FOR APPLICATION

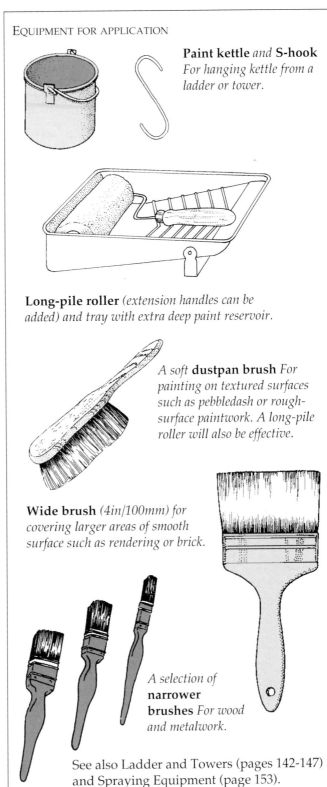

Paint kettle *and* **S-hook** *For hanging kettle from a ladder or tower.*

Long-pile roller *(extension handles can be added) and tray with extra deep paint reservoir.*

A soft **dustpan brush** *For painting on textured surfaces such as pebbledash or rough-surface paintwork. A long-pile roller will also be effective.*

Wide brush *(4in/100mm) for covering larger areas of smooth surface such as rendering or brick.*

A selection of **narrower brushes** *For wood and metalwork.*

See also Ladder and Towers (pages 142–147) and Spraying Equipment (page 153).

PAINT FOR WALLS

Sound brick walls are best left unpainted unless they have been repaired and patched with ugly and mismatched bricks. Once painted, brick walls will need to be re-painted every 4-7 years or so, and old wall paint is very difficult to remove.

Masonry paints: because they contain fibres or particles of sand, stone or granite they have a sufficiently thick texture to cover small cracks. Additives in the paint inhibit the growth of mould. They come in three textures – smooth, textured, and thick-bodied. Should last 4-7 years.

Outdoor emulsion paints: sold specifically for exterior use. They have additives to discourage mould growth. Should last 4-7 years.

Cement-based paint: not successful if applied over other paints. Cement-based paints are best used on new rendering or over an existing cement-based paint. They have a rough-textured finish and should last for 5-7 years. With age they may produce surface powder (see page 149).

Water-repellent coatings: a colourless liquid that will weatherproof walls for 5-10 years – but all cracks will need to be sealed first.

PAINT FOR WOODWORK

The best type of covering for exterior wood will depend on the appearance you want to achieve, and on the condition of the surface you intend to paint.

Paint: the choice is between traditional gloss paints (either liquid or non-drip) or special paints that are designed to allow the wood to expand and contract without cracking. Some special wood paints (called microporous or 'breathing' paints) allow moisture trapped in the wood to evaporate, thus preventing blistering (see page 148). If you are going to paint over existing paintwork, use the same kind of paint as used originally. You will not get the full benefit of special wood paint if it is painted over a traditional gloss. If bare wood is severely discoloured (say from burning-off scorches) it will have to be sealed with an aluminium-based primer. The primer will need at least three coats of undercoat.

Stains and varnishes: if you are working with new wood, or stripped raw wood, and want a natural finish, choose a varnish or protective wood stain specifically recommended for exterior use (generally, most interior wood stains are not suitable for exterior use, although there are now products which can be used indoors as well as out). For planed joinery use a microporous stain (i.e. one that allows air to pass through it).

HOW MUCH PAINT?

Different types of paint have different covering capacities. For example, non-drip paints do not cover as large an area as liquid paint, but their opacity (the density of their pigment) is greater, and therefore fewer coats will be needed. The covering capacity of paints will be stated on the tins and in literature available from the manufacturer or supplier. The amount of paint you will need will also be affected by the porosity of the surface you intend to paint. A previously painted surface will generally require less than new rendering. Because there are many variables to be considered, manufacturers give fairly wide ranges for coverage for traditional exterior masonry paint: 4-10 sq m per litre. A rule-of-thumb would be that 5 litres of paint will cover about 70 sq yds (58 sq m).

Calculating the area of wall to be covered is no different from that given on pages 26-27 for interior rooms. Drop a weighted string from the eaves to the ground and measure the string to determine the height of the walls. Using a steel tape measure is the easiest way to calculate the perimeter of the house. When both these measurements are multiplied together you will have the area to be painted (subtract about 2½ yd/2 sq m for each door and 1¾ sq yd/1.5 sq m for each window)

HOW MUCH TIME?

This will depend, obviously, on how much physical stamina you have as well as weather conditions (working for long hours in hot weather is definitely not a good idea, especially if you are not in good physical shape). Painting exteriors single-handed is physically demanding, and if you can enlist assistance you will cut down on time and effort considerably.

Excluding the time it takes to do major repairs, an average-sized house should take about two weeks to paint with a roller or brush (assuming there are no delays for bad weather). Spraying can cut the job down to a few days.

On a smooth, non-porous surface you should be able to cover approximately 13 sq yd (11 sq m) an hour with a 4in (100mm) brush. Pebbledash or heavily textured surfaces would take about 6 sq yd (5 sq m) per hour.

TIMING AND CONDITIONS

Although British summers can be notoriously fickle as far as weather is concerned, it is best to aim to paint exteriors towards the end of summer and beginning of autumn, based on the theory that exterior surfaces will have been thoroughly dried out. At the very least, you should allow two dry, warm days after any rain, fog or frost before painting outside. If you are unlucky enough to be caught by rain while you are painting, wait at least 24 hours before restarting. The surface has to be completely dry before resuming because paint applied to a wet or damp surface will flake or peel off.

If you are over-anxious to begin, you may find that moisture is trapped under the new paint, and this can lead to blistering and bubbling (see page 148). For the same reason, do not start painting until the morning dew has had time to evaporate.

The best conditions for painting outside are a warm temperature and an overcast sky. Do not paint directly under a hot sun. Not only is it uncomfortable, but the sun's rays will also dry out the surface of the paint too quickly, leaving the still-wet paint trapped underneath. Unless the paint is microporous, the trapped paint will cause blisters.

If at all possible, follow the sun around the building and paint on a surface that has been warmed, but not in direct sun.

Wind can be a problem, especially if you are using a paint-spraying machine or are at the top of a high ladder. It will blow dust on to wet paint, so if conditions are dry and dusty, spray the ground with water to reduce dust levels.

EQUIPMENT AND SAFETY

It is absolutely essential when working at height to use the safest equipment – and to use it safely. Most of the accidents that are caused when painting outside are due to the misuse of ladders. The pattern is depressingly repetitive: in the rush to get the job done, safety is shortcut. Instead of getting down from the ladder and moving it, we try and stretch just that little bit too far.

It is not expensive to hire good ladders and towers, and in terms of safety and convenience it simply is not worth improvising.

LADDERS

In order to reach the roof height of houses other than bungalows you will need an extending ladder. Wooden ladders are heavier than alloy ones, and are also more prone to wear. If you intend to use a wooden ladder, check carefully for loose or split rungs.

Extending ladders have double or even triple sections, and many use a rope and pulley system to extend sections. Remember, when calculating the length of ladder you require to add at least 2yd (2m) to accommodate the angle of lean. When extending the ladder, make sure the sections overlap by at least three rungs and that the retaining hooks are securely locked on to the relevant rung.

Ladders are divided into three categories by British Standards (BS2037 for aluminium ladders and BS1129 for wooden ones). The class of ladder designated by British Standards indicates the use for which it is most appropriate: class 1 (industrial), class 2 (light trade), and class 3 (domestic). In shops you may see them with colour-coded stickers for each category: blue for class 1, yellow for class 2, and red for class 3. You may also see ladders with British Ladder Manufacturers' Association stickers describing them as 'industrial', 'light trade' or 'domestic' – but this does not mean to say that ladders with these stickers are necessarily British Standards Institute approved.

Handling extending ladders
Extending ladders are heavy and unwieldy, so a few basic guidelines will help prevent unnecessary strains and injuries.

Raising an extending ladder

A. *Place the foot of the ladder up against the base of the wall, starting at the end furthest from the wall.*
B. *Raise the ladder and 'walk' your hands rung over rung towards the wall until the ladder is upright and leaning against the wall.*

C. Pull the foot of the ladder out from the wall until the distance from the wall is one quarter the height of the ladder. For example, a 20ft (6.6m) ladder should have its feet 5ft (1.6m) out from the wall. The ladder should lean at an angle of about 75°.

D. Extend the ladder (a much easier job if one person steadies it while the other either pushes the extension or raises it with the rope) and ensure the retaining hooks are properly locked on to the rung.

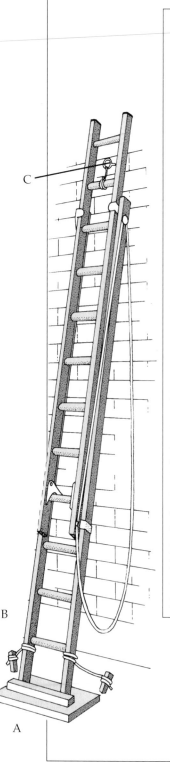

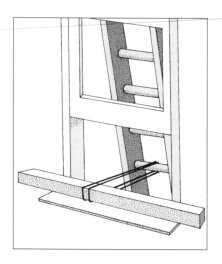

LADDER SAFETY

* Do not erect or use ladders in a high wind.

* Do not place ladders in front of a window or door that can open on to the ladder.

* Do not over-reach. Get down and move the ladder.

* Make sure the ladder extends at least five or six rungs higher than the level at which you will stand.

* Always keep one hand on the ladder when working.

* If the ground is soft you will need to put the ladder on a stable base. Make a footing plate from a piece of board with a batten fixed at the back to prevent the ladder slipping off (A).

* Secure the ladder by driving pegs into the ground and lashing the ladder to them (B).

* If the masonry below the roof line is solid, fix ring bolts at intervals and secure the top of the ladder to them with rope (C).

* Lash the ladder to a piece of plank or stout timber that straddles the inside of a window frame. The wood should project at least 12in (30cm) beyond the window's sides. Wrap the ends of the wood in cloth to protect interior paintwork.

* Never secure a ladder to guttering or pipes (particularly plastic).

* If the ladder is going to stand on a hard surface such as concrete or paving, attach adjustable rubber-soled feet to the ladder to prevent slipping.

* Never leave a ladder unattended if there are children around. Drop it to the horizontal when not in use.

* Do not erect a ladder near overhead electrical cables.

* Check wooden ladders for loose, broken or missing rungs. Never paint wooden ladders as it can hide defects. Varnish them if necessary.

Ladder accessories

Safety and convenience go hand in hand. If you are distracted by not having tools within reach and tired of constantly going up and down the ladder to fetch them, you are more likely to take a shortcut on safety.

There is a range of add-ons that can help with problems. Ladder-stays fix on to the top of the ladder and hold it away from the wall. Not only does a stay help stabilise the ladder, but it also keeps it off guttering that can be damaged or give way. A stay enables the ladder to clear overhanging eaves.

Clip-on tool trays keep smaller tools handy, while S-hooks enable you to hang the paint container within easy reach.

Adjustable feet can be bolted on to provide a safer purchase on uneven ground. Standing platforms clip on to rungs to give a more comfortable perch than a narrower rung.

Standing platforms clip on to rungs to give a more comfortable footing than a narrow rung.

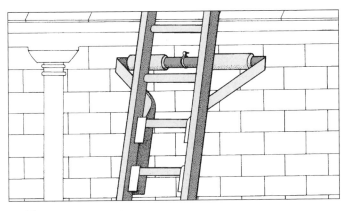

Ladder stays.

Adjustable feet.

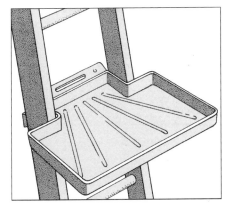

Above: *Clip-on tool tray.*

Right: *Standing platform.*

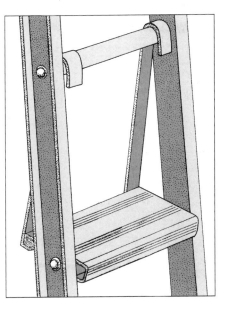

ACCESS TOWERS

An alternative to a ladder for tackling high jobs is an access (or platform) tower which is made up from interlocking metal sections topped off with a wooden platform. A typical tower will provide a working platform area of around 4 x 4ft (1.2 x 1.2m) with a typical maximum platform height of around 16ft (5m) without outriggers stabilising the base. With stabilising outriggers some platforms can be raised to over 30ft (10m).

Tower accessories

Access towers are supplied in kit form. The basic components are H-shaped units, diagonal braces and guard rails. In addition you will need:

Platform boards to make the platform floor, and toe-boards (like a low wooden wall) that go round the edge of the platform and prevent tools and suchlike from being accidentally kicked off the platform.

Outriggers (or stabilisers) will need to be fitted to the base if you intend to build higher than the manufacturer's recommended maximum height unstabilised.

Base plates give the tower feet a firm footing, and some are adjustable to cope better with uneven ground. Alternatively, castors in place of base plates are useful if you need to move the tower frequently and if it is standing on something as solid as concrete. The castors should be lockable.

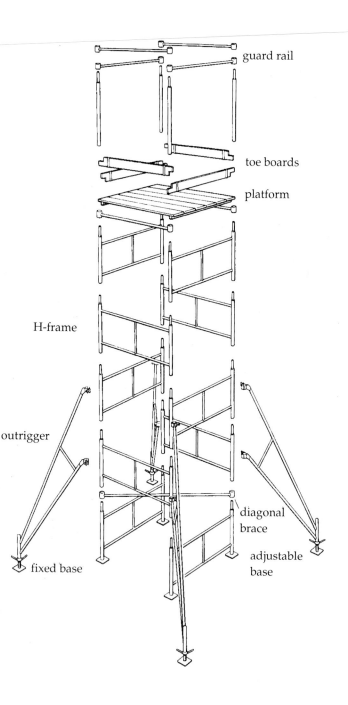

guard rail

toe boards

platform

H-frame

outrigger

diagonal brace

adjustable base

fixed base

* The maximum platform height of an access tower should not exceed three times the smaller base dimension, or three times the effective base size when using outriggers.

* Make sure you have enough room for the outriggers before you start erecting.

* Provide additional support by lashing the tower to ring bolts in the wall, or securing it with a plank straddling the inside of a window (see page 144). Never lash a tower to a drain-pipe or guttering.

* Erect the tower on firm and level foundations. On soft ground use base plates nailed to large wooden boards to spread the load. Use adjustable bases on uneven ground.

* Make sure castors are locked before using the tower.

* Make sure that each section is securely fitted together and where possible bring up platform boards to stand on as you erect the next stage.

* Only climb up a ladder that has been securely lashed to the inside of the frame. Carry tools up in a bag or belt in order to leave both hands free for a ladder. Do not lean a ladder against the tower.

* Do not overload the platform or use it as a base for a ladder. Do not lean a ladder against the tower.

* Never leave the tower unattended if there are children around.

* Bring platform boards down when the tower is not being used. High winds can lift them off.

LADDERS V. TOWERS

Ladders are easy to put up and move around, and allow you to get up to inaccessible areas relatively easily. They don't need much storage space. Accidents, however, are common, and the need to hold on with one hand and the lack of space on which to rest tools, etc, limits what you can do from a ladder. In addition they are uncomfortable to stand on for any length of time.

Access towers are safe and stable when assembled correctly, provide a large working platform, and leave both hands free. Sections can be added to extend the tower over roofs (to reach chimneys for example). However, the size of the tower limits its use and it is much more cumbersome to erect than a ladder.

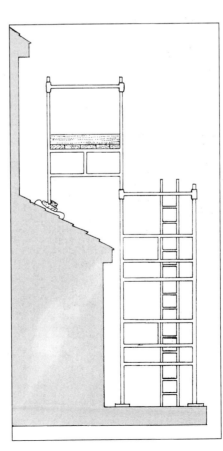

Cantilevered sections afford access over extension roofs. Sandbags and boards under the feet of the cantilevered section help protect the roof. The ladder is inside the tower. Never lean a ladder against the outside of a tower or use the platform as a base for a ladder.

COMMON PROBLEMS

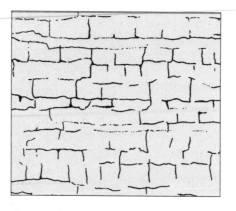

ALLIGATORING

As the name suggests, the paint has cracked in a scale-like pattern resembling alligator skin. Alligatoring is caused either by applying a second coat of paint before the first has dried thoroughly, thus trapping the moisture from the first coat, or by applying a second coat which is incompatible with the first. Alligatoring allows water to penetrate the wood through the cracks in the paint. The paint will have to be stripped right back to bare wood.

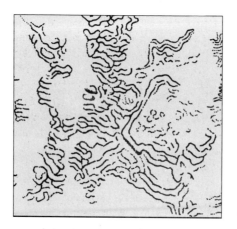

WRINKLING

If paint (particularly oil-based paint) is applied too thickly, the surface film dries and traps wet paint underneath. The paint then sags into into wrinkles. If the paint under the wrinkles is still wet, the wrinkles should be scraped off. When the paint has dried thoroughly it should be rubbed down with sandpaper before repainting. If the wrinkles are hard, they will have to be sanded smooth or burned and scraped off. Use a thinner paint when re-coating, and brush it in thoroughly to avoid further wrinkling.

BLISTERING AND PEELING

If moisture or solvent is trapped under the paint it will prevent the paint adhering to the surface. Blistering and peeling are more commonly problems of oil-based paints that have been applied under a hot sun. The surface film of the paint dries very quickly, trapping solvent underneath. It can also be caused by painting on to damp wood. Strip the paint back to bare wood and make sure the underlying wood is thoroughly dry before repainting. Avoid painting in the full glare of the sun.

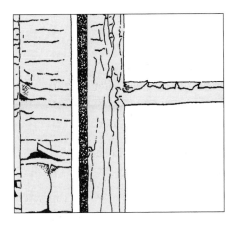

PEELING FROM WOOD

Paint cannot adhere to wood that is damp, greasy, dirty or still has flaky old paint. Any old paint must be scraped off and the wood thoroughly prepared (see page 150) before repainting. If the wood is damp, the source of the damp must be eliminated and the wood allowed to dry out completely.

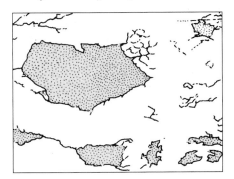

PEELING FROM MASONRY

As with wood, paint will peel from brick and rendering if the wall was damp or dirty, but it will also peel if it has been undermined by alkali deposits in the masonry. All the flaking paint will have to be scraped off and the masonry stabilised with an alkali-resistant sealer or masonry paint with alkali-resistant properties.

OOZING KNOTS

If you paint over knots that are still 'live' (i.e. those in which the resin has not been allowed to dry out) there is a good chance that the resin will bleed out and stain and blister the paintwork. Strip off the paint to expose the knot. Using a hot-air gun or blowtorch, heat the knot until all the resin has bubbled out. Scrape off the resin and seal the knot with shellac knotting solution or an aluminium wood primer.

EFFLORESCENCE

Paint will blister and disintegrate when mineral salts present in masonry are activated by dampness. Efflorescence is the term given to the white powdery blisters caused by this chemical reaction. Do not try and wash it off, as water only makes matters worse. Brush off as much of the powdery residue as possible and tackle the damp problem before attempting the repaint.

MOULD

Damp and shade are the favoured conditions for the growth of fungal spores and algae. Mould cannot be removed simply by brushing it off because the spores will grow back. They must be killed with a fungicide (there are proprietary brands, but a solution of 1 part household bleach to 4 parts warm water is also effective). Scrub the sterilising solution vigorously into the affected area and leave for 48 hours. Wash with clean water and allow the affected area to dry out completely. As damp is one cause of mould and algae, check for leaking pipes and gutters or dripping overflow pipes in particular. Use a paint containing a fungicide.

PREPARATION

ORDER OF EVENTS

Professional painters and decorators tackle a house in a set order. Essentially the rules are: work from large areas to small (walls before trim) and work from the top to the bottom. On a typical house the order of painting would be:
1. Fascia and barge boards.
2. Gutters.
3. Walls.
4. Windows and doors.
5. Drainpipes.
The same order of events should be followed for preparation, priming and undercoating, as well as for finishing.

PREPARING WALLS

Brickwork should only need painting if repairs have left ugly patches of mismatched bricks, or if new bricks are of a particularly raw and ugly colour. Brush the brickwork with a stiff brush, Repoint the mortar if necessary. If the surface of the brickwork is particularly crumbly or has been previously painted with cement paint that has powdered with age, seal the surface by brushing on a proprietary stabilising solution. See page 149 for dealing with efflorescence.

Rendering, whether it is smooth, textured or pebbledashed, should be brushed down with a stiff brush. Take care to brush out any loose debris from cracks. Repair cracks and holes with ready-mixed mortar or an exterior-grade filling compound. If the surface of the rendering is particularly crumbly, or has been previously painted with a cement paint that has become powdery with age, brush on a proprietary stabilising solution. For treatment of mould and for peeling paint, see page 149.

PREPARING WOODWORK

If the existing paintwork is in good condition it will only need to be lightly rubbed down with sandpaper to key the surface for the new paint, then wiped over with a solution of sugar soap to remove all grease, dirt and salt deposits. Isolated patches of chipped or flaked paint can be filled with exterior-grade filling compound or waterproof stopping compound which, when dried, should be rubbed down to the level of the surrounding paintwork and then primed.

If the paintwork is extensively damaged it will have to be stripped back to the bare wood. Use the hot-air gun or blowtorch technique described on page 38. Sand the bare wood and seal any knots (see page 34). Prime the bare wood with an aluminium wood primer and undercoat in preparation for the finishing coat.

WINDOWS

If putty has dried out and is cracked or lifting, it should be raked out, taking care not to dislodge the pins that hold the pane in place. Brush out any loose debris and dust.

If whole runs of putty need to be replaced, first prime the rebates. This will make it easier for the putty to adhere. Take a ball of fresh putty and work it in your hands until it becomes soft and pliable. Lay strips of putty about ¼in (6mm) thick into the rebates and smooth it with a narrow filling knife held at an angle to give a neat bevelled edge. Make sure the putty does not come so far up the pane that it is visible from the inside of the window. Finally, run a finger wrapped in damp cloth lightly along the putty to smooth the surface.

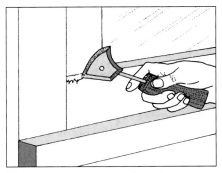

Using a shavehook to rake out old putty.

Corner joints are the most commonly damaged parts of the window frame and should be raked out with a shavehook or knife. Brush out any debris and fill with putty, exterior-grade filler or stopping compound. When the filler is dry, rub down with sandpaper and prime.

Gaps between window and door frames and surrounding masonry should be sealed with an appropriate mastic.

PREPARING METALWORK

Old guttering and pipework made from ferrous metal are particularly prone to rusting. It is essential to remove all old flaking paint and rust, either by using a combination of wire brush, scraper and emery paper or by using wire-brush attachments to an electric drill. The drill method speeds up the job but it is important to wear goggles and a dust mask.

Wire brushing to remove old paint and rust.

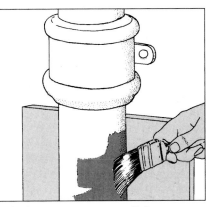

Painting on a rust-neutralising solution.

Once the metal is rust free (really deep-seated rust can be treated with a rust-neutralising solution available from DIY outlets) it is important to prime it as quickly as possible with red lead or zinc chromate primer. Ferrous metal will re-rust very quickly if left unprotected.

PLASTIC PIPE AND GUTTERING

Plastic pipes and gutters will usually be left in their original grey or black finish. But if you want to paint them, first wipe over with white spirit to clean off any grease and dirt. When the surface is dry, use an oil-based paint.

PAINTING WALLS

BRUSHING

If the surface is of relatively smooth brick or rendering, use a 4in (100mm) brush. Anything wider makes for heavy work when the brush is loaded with paint. If the surface is textured, an ordinary household dust-pan brush will effectively get paint into crevices. You can also buy brushes specially designed for rough surfaces. Whichever you choose, keep it well loaded with paint so that small cracks and crevices are filled.

ROLLERS

A roller with a long pile will be needed for exterior walls (and for pebbledash an extra-long pile will be needed to get into the nooks and crannies between pebbles). An extension pole that screws into the handle of the roller and a tray with an extra-deep paint reservoir will be very useful additions when working from the ground or the platform of an access tower. Working with a roller from a ladder is not easy, however, and a special roller bucket which holds 10 litres of paint would be a good investment. A piece of board inside the kettle will help to take off excess paint from the roller.

WINDOWS AND DOORS

The sequence for painting the exterior faces of windows and doors is the same as that used on interiors (see page 47 for windows, and page 46 for doors).

Make sure you do not fill the grooves that run underneath window sills with paint. If they are blocked, rainwater will run back to the wall rather than dripping off the front lip of the sill.

Start at the top of the wall and, using a 2-3in (50-75mm) brush, cut in around the edges.

Fill the area not outlined with a larger brush or roller. Move across the wall in horizontal bands: right-to-left if you are right-handed; left-to-right if left-handed.

SPRAYING WALLS

Spraying comes into its own only if you have relatively large areas of wall to cover. Although spraying is certainly quicker and less physically demanding than wielding a brush or roller, a considerable amount of time will have to be spent carefully masking off those areas such as windows, pipes and doors that you do not want sprayed.

SPRAYING EQUIPMENT

Many tool hire shops rent paint-spraying equipment, and it is important to explain to them the kind of job you need the sprayer to tackle. Some, for example, cannot handle textured paint. Make sure that you have been given adequate instructions on setting-up, operating and cleaning the equipment.

Airless sprayers

Paint is drawn up from a separate container (usually an ordinary bucket or paint kettle) and is pumped at very high pressure to be released as spray through the nozzle of a gun when you pull the trigger.

Airless sprayers cannot handle textured paint, and all paint should be strained (through an old piece of nylon stocking, for example).

Because the airless sprayer delivers paint at very high pressure and speed it can cover areas quickly (about 240 sq yd/200 sq m per hour) but there are attendant risks. Paint delivered at such pressure can be injected through the skin if it is accidentally sprayed at close range. If you do spray yourself at close range, seek immediate medical attention. Always follow the safety precautions suggested by the manufacturer or hire shop and read the safety points in the box on the following page.

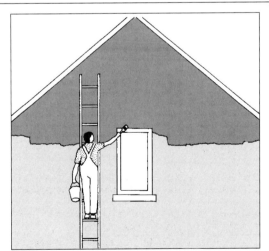

As you work down from roof height, cut in around windows with the smaller brush.

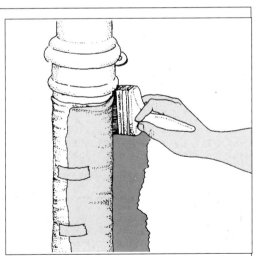

Protect pipework by wrapping it in old newspaper or plastic sheeting so that you can brush in behind it.

Compressed-air sprayers

A compressor delivers pressurised air to the spray gun where it mixes with the paint (usually contained in a reservoir attached to the gun) and comes out of the nozzle as fine spray when the trigger is pulled. The pressures involved are not as great as those from an airless sprayer

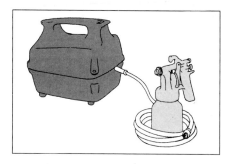

and so coverage is generally slower. The relatively small paint container (usually less than 2 pints/1 litre) means more frequent refills than an airless sprayer.

Whether using airless or compressed-air sprayers, check that the nozzle is suitable for the type of paint you intend to use.

Masking

Windows, doors and pipework will have to be carefully masked off with sheets of paper or polythene and masking tape. Use drop-cloths on the ground at the foot of the wall.

SAFE SPRAYING

* Never point the spray gun at anyone and keep hands away from the nozzle.

* Check that the gun has a safety shield around the nozzle, as well as a trigger guard and lock.

* Always lock the trigger of the gun when putting it down, passing it to someone, or leaving it unattended. Also make sure the trigger is locked before making any adjustments to the gun or spray tip.

* Always wear goggles and a face mask.

* Never leave spraying equipment unattended when children are around.

* Do not smoke when spraying. Atomised oil paint spray is highly toxic if inhaled with hot smoke.

* Always unplug the pump and release pressure from the hose by squeezing the trigger before cleaning the equipment.

* Never try to clear blocked nozzles while machine is running.

Spraying techniques

Get a feel for the sprayer by testing it on a piece of cardboard or board. It will also give you an opportunity to adjust the consistency of the paint so that it sprays evenly.

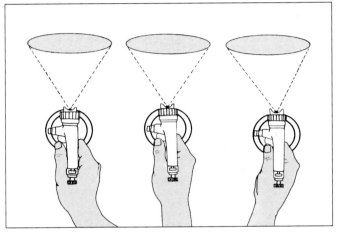

Wrist-action keeps spray-gun parallel to surface.

Move along surface in horizontal bands.

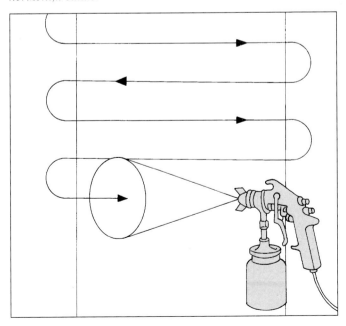

1. Hold the gun about 10-12in (250-300mm) from the wall.
2. Make sure the gun is perpendicular to the wall. It is important to try and keep this parallel distance as you move along the wall in order to get an even finish. If you swing the gun in an arc, or tilt it up or down you will get an uneven spread of paint.
3. Move along the surface in horizontal bands, overlapping each stroke to compensate for the lighter coverage at the edges of the fan of spray.
4. To get an even beginning and end to each strip, spray a little distance beyond each end of the strip.

Spraying problems

Spattering Too high pressure may produce a speckled surface.

Wrinkling Paint sprayed on too thickly will sag into runs and wrinkles. Either the consistency of the paint needs to be thinned a little or you are moving the gun too slowly and causing a build up of paint.

Clogging If the paint is spluttering and spitting it is probably due to a partially clogged nozzle. Never attempt to clear a blocked nozzle while the machine is running. Turn it off and release any pressure remaining in the hose. Clean the nozzle with the appropriate solvent (white spirit for oil-based paint; water for water-based paint) and a brush (an old toothbrush is useful). Do not poke wire into the nozzle.

Cleaning the equipment

Always clean the equipment thoroughly after each day's work or if you have to leave it for an extended break. Empty the paint container and spray out any paint remaining in the hose. Put solvent into the paint container and spray out the solvent (on to a piece of cardboard, for example) until the hoses and nozzle have been thoroughly flushed through and cleaned.

GLOSSARY

Acrylic paint A plastic-like resin binds the pigments, driers and solvents in latex paint.

Alkyd paint An oil-based paint made with synthetic alkyd resins. Most modern interior oil-based paints are alkyds.

Alligatoring Paint that has dried and cracked in a scale-like pattern resembling alligator skin. Caused by applying a second coat of paint over an insufficiently dried first coat, or over an incompatible paint.

Barge boards The wooden trim at the ends of a roof.

Binders See Resins.

Blanket stripper A chemical paste used to lift off old paint.

Booking Folding pasted wallcovering in concertina-fashion for easier carrying and handling.

Bridging boards Stout planks lashed or clamped between stepladders to provide a working platform.

Butt seams Where the edges of the wallcovering to be joined meet flush without overlapping. (See also Double-cut seams).

Casement windows Often made of metal, casement windows open with a door-like movement. (See also Sash windows).

Caustic soda An extremely powerful and corrosive paint stripper made from sodium hydroxide.

Complementary colours Those colours opposite each other on the colour wheel. (See page 11.)

'Cool' colours Those of the blue-green sector of the colour spectrum. (See also 'Warm' colours).

Cornice A decorative rail-like moulding, usually of plaster, that runs around a room just below the ceiling.

Counterpunch A steel punch used to sink protruding nailheads below the surface. Counterpunching nails is particularly important before sanding a floor.

Crown moulding A decorative trim, usually of plaster, that runs along the join between wall and ceiling.

Cutting-in Using a relatively narrow brush to paint the edges of a wall or ceiling before filling in the larger expanse with a wider brush or roller.

Dado rail A decorative moulding, usually of plaster or wood, that runs along the wall at about waist height.

Distemper An old-fashioned paint made of chalk, gum and water. Old distemper should be washed off with water.

Distressing A term used for special paint techniques such as dragging, ragging or stippling where a top coat is either partially removed or applied without covering the entire surface in order to allow some of the underlying base coat to show through the 'distressed' final coat.

Double-cut seams A technique of joining wallcovering by overlapping the edges of adjacent strips and cutting through the centre of the overlap. The cut strips are removed to leave a neat butt join. (See also Butt seam).

Dowel A cylindrical length of wood, sometimes cut in half or quarters down its length.

DPC Acronym for damp-proof course: a water-proof barrier of plastic sheet, mortar or slate that runs between two courses of brick (usually about two courses up from ground level) that prevents rising damp.

Dragging A special paint or 'distressing' technique in which a relatively dry brush is dragged through a top coat of glaze, thus allowing some of the underlying base coat to show through.

Eccentric sander An electrically powered wood sander with a sanding plate that not only revolves but also oscillates at high speed.

Edging sander A small electrically powered wood sander for getting in closer to walls and skirtingboard than could be managed with a large drum sander. (See also Eccentric sander and Orbital sander).

Efflorescence The reaction in masonry of mineral salts and damp which causes paint to blister and powder.

Eggshell finish A trade term used to describe the low-sheen finish available in some oil-based paints.

Emulsion paint A water-based, virtually odour-free paint most commonly used for quick drying and inexpensive coverage of interior walls and ceilings. It can be bought in liquid and 'solid' (gel-like) forms.

Fascia boards The wooden boards that run along exterior walls just below the roof to which guttering is attached.

Flagging The split ends of each bristle of a paint brush. The more flagging, the more paint a brush can hold.

Flaunching The sloping mortar base in which a chimney pot is seated.

Flush door Doors with a flat surface uninterrupted by raised or recessed panels. (See also Panel door).

Glaze A mixture of oil and mineral spirits which is coloured with a small amount of artists' oil colour before being used in special paint techniques such as rag-rolling or dragging. (See also Scumble glaze).

Grinning A term used to describe the show-through of underlying colours that results when the covering paint has been over-thinned or inadequately mixed so that pigments and solvent have not been sufficiently emulsified.

Grout A paste-like compound used to fill in the joins between ceramic tiles.

Knotting A solution of shellac resin and white spirit used to seal knots in wood that are still actively oozing resin.

Latex paint A paint in which the pigments and other ingredients are suspended in water.

Lining paper Rolls of cheap off-white paper used to cover a surface and act as a clean, firm base for the final wallcovering.

Lint-free rag A cotton-based cleaning cloth which does not shed fibre particles into wet paint or varnish (as opposed to, for example, a linen rag which is made from flax).

Marbling A special paint technique that imitates the veining and colouration of natural marble.

Mastic A type of filler which, because of a degree of elasticity when dry, is particularly useful in filling joins that may be subject to slight expansion-contraction movement.

Microporous paint A paint that 'breathes', allowing moisture trapped beneath the surface of the paint to escape.

Nibs The sharp little peaks of hardened paint, most often found when working with gloss or textured paint.

Orbital sander An electrically powered wood sander with a sanding plate that revolves at high speed. Used mainly as an edging sander.

Panel door A traditional door with recessed or raised panels. (See also Flush door).

Pigment Particles suspended in a solution of water or oil that give paint its colour and opacity.

Plumb bob/plumb line A length of string with a weight at one end. It is held up or fixed to a wall so that the weight is freely suspended. When the weight has come to a complete standstill the string forms a truly vertical line.

Primary colours The source of all colours: red, blue, yellow. (See Secondary colours and Tertiary colours).

Primer A preparatory covering of paint that reduces the absorbency of the surface. The primer may be the finishing paint itself, thinned with water or spirit (whichever is used in the finishing paint). Ready-made primer is usually much cheaper than finishing paint.

Primer-sealer A combination of sealer to prevent stains leaching out of the surface into the top-coat paint, and primer to bond to the surface to prevent too much paint being absorbed into the surface.

Profile gauge A gauge containing rows of movable pins which, when pushed up against, for example, the moulding of a door frame, take on the contours of the moulding. The pins can then be locked and the contour outline traced on to a tile, for example, so that when the tile is cut it will butt up to the moulding accurately.

PVA A milky and near-odourless adhesive used primarily in woodworking, PVA is also sometimes added to colour washes, for example, to give them extra durability when dry.

Radiator brush A narrow brush-head mounted on to a long, angled handle for easier access to the gap between the back of a radiator and the wall.

Ragging A special paint technique in which a bunched rag is used to apply (in ragging-on) or remove (in ragging-off) a top coat of glaze or paint, thus allowing irregular areas of underlying base coat to show through.

Rebate The inside plane of a window cross-rail, where the pane meets the rail.

Related colours Those colours next to each other on the colour wheel. (See page 11).

Resins Those elements in a paint's composition that form the thin yet durable and flexible surface film that holds the pigment. Resins used to be made from vegetable and insect extracts, but today they are made chiefly from chemicals such as acrylic, alkyd, vinyl and urethane. Resins are also known as 'binders' because they bind pigment.

Sash windows The more traditional two- part window construction where each part slides up and down. (See also Casement window).

Scumble glaze A transparent oil glaze, thinned with white spirit and coloured with small amounts of artists' colours and used in a variety of special paint techniques such as dragging and stippling.

Sealer A solution used to seal porous surfaces such as bare wood, plaster or masonry and prevent stains leaching out from the surface and contaminating the top-coat paint.

Seam roller A narrow wooden or plastic-headed roller used to flatten the joined edges of wallcovering.

Secondary colours The result of an equal mix of any two primary colours. (See Primary colours and Tertiary colours).

Shavehook A hand scraper with a flat triangular-shaped head used for removing paint lodged in wood moulding.

Shellac A traditional varnish which when mixed with white spirits is one of the ingredients in knotting, a solution used to seal resinous wood knots.

Size A glue-like wash traditionally used to prime a surface before wallpapering in order to reduce the absorbancy of the surface.

Skirtingboard A wooden board that runs along the foot of an interior wall.

Sleeve The fleece or foam-rubber cover that slides over the metal cage of a paint roller.

Soffit The underside of, for example, a door lintel, architrave, cornice, or a roof rafter where it overhangs a wall.

Solvent To enable the constituent elements of paint, e.g. pigments, resins, and plasticisers, to be liquid enough for application to a surface they need to be held in some kind of solution. For oil-based paint it is usually white spirit (older oil paints used turpentine), and for emulsion paint it is water. After the paint has been applied the solvent evaporates to leave the pigment held in a resin film on the surface.

Sponging A special paint technique in which glaze or paint is applied (sponging-on) or partially removed (sponging-off) thus allowing the underlying base coat to show through.

Stippling A special paint technique in which a top coat or flake or paint is dabbed on to a dried on to a dried base coat using the tips of a brush's bristles. The base coat shows through the dot-like top coat.

Straightedge A longish ruler-like length of metal or wood used for marking out a straight line.

Sugar soap A cleaning agent (trisodium phosphate) used for washing down paintwork prior to repainting.

Tack cloth A lint-free cloth impregnated with linseed oil used to remove dust specks from a surface about to be glossed, varnished or polyurethaned.

Tertiary colours The result of mixing two secondary colours. (See Secondary colours and Primary colours).

Tone A colour's relative lightness or darkness. A tint is achieved by adding white; a shade by adding black.

Undercoat A preliminary coat of paint used to give depth and density to the finishing coat by obliterating the existing colour of the surface.

Universal tiles Ceramic wall or floor tiles with bevelled edges that ensure automatic spacing.

Varnish A protective coating (essentially a paint without pigment) that is usually made from polyurethane resins and dries to a hard finish. Some varnishes come as two interactive components that have to be mixed to create an even tougher finish than the more common ready-to-use types.

'Warm' colours Those from the yellow-red sector of the colour wheel. (See page 11).

Washes Paint or glaze thinned almost to the point of translucency. When brushed over a dried base coat the thinness of the wash allows the base coat to show through.

Wet-and-dry paper A type of abrasive paper that needs to be lubricated with water.

Wrinkling A common problem with oil paint that has been applied too thickly. The still- wet drags into folds and dries into hardened wrinkles.

INDEX